Lost Coast Review
Spring 2015
Volume 6, Number 3

Cover Image: Boston Harbor Lighthouse by Alan Wood
http://www.123rf.com/profile_alwoodphoto'>alwoodphoto /
123RF Stock Photo</a> with permission

AVIGNON PRESS
Newport Beach, CA, USA
ISBN: 978-0692422038
ISSN: 2332-4805

Lost Coast Review

Volume 6, Number 3, Spring 2015

Editorial Staff

Editor-in-Chief	Casey Dorman
Associate Editor	Darryl Freeland
Book Review Editor	Noel Mawer
Film Review Editor	Hadley Hury
Poetry Editor	Randall Mawer
Short Story Editor	Diane Rogers
Business/Marketing Mgr.	Lai Le Dorman

Publisher: Avignon Press

LOST COAST REVIEW (ISSN 2332-4805) is published quarterly by AVIGNON PRESS, at 41 Shearwater Place, Newport Beach, CA 92660. Lost Coast Review welcomes unsolicited submissions of short stories, poetry, book and film reviews. Please see submissions page for instructions on submissions. Subscriptions of Lost Coast Review may be purchased for $20/year (plus postage). Subscriptions and individual copies of Lost Coast Review may be purchased through the publisher's website at www.avignonpress.com or by accessing the online version at www.lostcoastreview.com

Contents

Contributors

Ivan Alexander (Short Story: *The Red Light*) is a world traveler who infuses his writing with wonder, realism, and heart. Ivan's interests range from history and culture to science and philosophy. His professional career focused on investment with a Wall Street bank. He splits his time between Orange County, California, and Rome, Italy, with his wife Cinzia. He has previously published in *Lost Coast Review*.

Daniel Barbare (Three Poems) has had poems recently appear in *The Santa Clara Review, Doxa, Blood* and *Thunder, Dewpoint, Watershed, The Round, Huizache, Clare Literary Magazine, Assisi Online Journal*, as well as many more online and print journals. He resides in Greenville, SC with his wife and family.

Les Bohem *(*Short Story: *Beatle Boots*) wrote the screenplay *Twenty Bucks*, based on a 1935 script by his father, Endre, (they are credited as co-writers). The movie earned critical praise and several awards, including an Independent Spirit Award. His other screenwriting credits include *Daylight, Dante's Peak, The Alamo, Kid, Nowhere To Run, The Darkest Hour* and the mini-series, *Taken* which he wrote and executive produced (with Steven Spielberg) and for which he won an Emmy award. His band, Gleaming Spires, had a cultish hit with their single, "Are You Ready For the Sex Girls," (featured in *Revenge of the Nerds*). He's also written songs recorded by Emmylou Harris, Randy Travis, Freddy Fender, and others. His short novel, *Flight 505*, will be published by UpperRubberBoot next year and his latest story, *Geister*, is included in Blumhouse books inaugural offering, *Book of Horrors*, due out in July.

Heidi C. Bowerman (Short Story: *If Only…*) is an award-winning playwright. Produced plays include *Rule #1; Denial;* and *My Hero*— winner of the Zeitgeist Theatre Company's Annual Rorschach Award for "the play with the most twists." When she is not writing, she is planning her escape from the mental hospital—for convicted sex offenders—where she works as a doctor of psychology.

Tobi Cogswell (Poetry: "Inattentive You") is a five-time Pushcart nominee and a Best of the Net nominee. Her seventh and latest chapbook is *The Coincidence of Castles* from Glass Lyre Press. Her collaborative full-length collection, *The Color of Forgiveness*, is available from Mojave River Press. She is the co-editor of *San Pedro River Review*.

Darren Demaree (Poetry: "Folds") poems have appeared, or are scheduled to appear in numerous magazines/journals, including the *South Dakota Review*, *Meridian*, *The Louisville Review*, *Grist*, and the *Colorado Review*. He is the author of *As We Refer To Our Bodies* (2013, 8th House), *Temporary Champions* (2014, Main Street Rag), and *Not For Art Nor Prayer* (2015, 8th House). He is the Managing Editor of the *Best of the Net Anthology*. He is currently living and writing in Columbus, Ohio with his wife and children.

Casey Dorman (Book Review: *Einstein's Beach House*) is the Editor-in-Chief of *Lost Coast Review*.

Robin Wyatt Dunn (Short Story: *Need*) writes and teaches in Los Angeles. His sixth novel, *Conquistador Of The Night Lands* , is due out from Villipede Press later this year

Alex Hughes (Three Poems) Alex Hughes lives and works in Los Angeles. He splits his time, depending on his mood and the weather, between his training in clinical psychology, his research in existential crises, and his fiction, poetry, and sketching. Sometimes, however, he does absolutely nothing, and he enjoys that time the most. These are his first published poems.

Hadley Hury (Film Review: "Five for Summer") has had his poetry and short fiction appear in *Forge Journal*, *Off the Coast*, *Appalachian Heritage*, *The James Dickey Review*, *Colorado Review*, *Avatar*, *Image*, *Green Mountains Review* and numerous other journals, reviews, and magazines. He has published a novel and a collection of short stories, and was for ten years film critic for *The Memphis Flyer*. He has also been an associate professor in film at the University of Memphis and lecturer in film at Rhodes College, The Memphis College of Art, and the Brooks Museum. A former teacher and senior executive for not-for-profit organizations focusing on the environment and women's health, he lives with his wife Marilyn in Louisville, Kentucky. Hadley is the Film Review Editor for *Lost Coast Review*.

J.H. Johns (Two Poems) "grew up and came of age" while living in East Tennessee and Middle Georgia. and currently lives in upstate New York where when he is not writing, he tends to his "nature preserve" and his "back forty." Most recently his work has appeared in *The East Coast Literary Review, Exercise Bowler, Four and Twenty, Commonline, Danse Macabre Du Jour* (2), *The West Wind Review, The Potomac, Syndic Literary Journal* (5), *Smokebox, Word Slaw, Wizards of the Wind, Alura,* and is forthcoming in *Syndic Literary Journal,* and *ken*again.*

Peycho Kanev (Two Poems) is the author of 4 poetry collections and two chapbooks. He has won several European awards for his poetry and been nominated for a Pushcart Award and Best of the Net. Translations of his books will be published soon in Italy, Poland and Russia. His poems have appeared in more than 1000 literary magazines, such as: *Poetry Quarterly, Evergreen Review, Hawaii Review, Cordite Poetry Review, Sheepshead Review, Off the Coast, The Adirondack Review, The Coachella Review, Two Thirds North, Sierra Nevada Review, The Cleveland Review* and many others.

Mark Mansfield (Five Poems) has appeared in numerous publications, including *The Adirondack Review, Bayou, Blue Mesa Review, The Evansville Review, Fourteen Hills, Gargoyle, The Ledge, Limestone, Magma, Salt Hill, Scrivener Creative Review, Tulane Review,* and *Unsplendid.* He holds an M.A. in Writing from Johns Hopkins. Currently, he lives in upstate New York where he teaches, works in a factory, and dreams of saving enough money to buy a new muffler for his car.

Michael Mark (Three Poems) is a hospice volunteer and long distance walker. His poetry has appeared or is forthcoming in *Gargoyle Magazine, Gravel Literary Journal, Lost Coast Review, Prelude Magazine, Rattle, Spillway, Tar River Poetry* and other nice places. His poetry has been nominated for a Pushcart Prize.

William Miller (Two Poems) is a widely-published poet and children's author. His poems have appeared in such places as *The Southern Review, The South Carolina Review* and *West Branch.* He lives in the French Quarter of New Orleans.

R.A. Morean (Short Story: *Parades*) has published dozens of short stories and essays in *Ploughshares, Kalliope, Mused, The Tishman Review,* and more. A *Salon* contributor, articles have included issues relating to atheism, digital media, parenting and education. She is president of the nationally acclaimed Antioch Writers' Workshop, and has published three novels with St. Martin's Press (US) and Breese Books (UK) under the pseudonym Abbey Pen Baker about the daughter of Sherlock Holmes. Escape Press (Harlequin AU) is releasing a romcom, *We've Got This,* in summer 2015, and Double Life Press will release *Being God (and other unfortunate avocations),* a literary novel, in 2016. A professor at Sinclair College, she also teaches creative writing workshops throughout the Miami Valley.

Frank Pray (Short Story: *Family Honor*) Frank Pray has written numerous poems, several short stories, and a novella. He began writing seriously about 3 years ago, and is focused on building his craft. His genres include detective, romance, science fiction, and currently a longer work about a woman who becomes head of the Catholic Church. He lives in Irvine California. His poetry has appeared in *Lost Coast Review.*

Ndaba Sibanda (Poetry: "Food For Thought") is a Zimbabwean-born writer. He hails from Bulawayo, Zimbabwe`s second largest city. In 2005 he authored an epic, *Love O'clock.* He has since contributed to fifteen published books including such international anthologies as *Poems For Haiti, A South African anthology, Snippets, Voices Of Peace, Black Communion, Ripples of Love, Lost Coast Review, Summer 2014: Vol. 5, No. 3, On the Rusk Issue Three (Volume 3), Emanations: Foray into Forever, World Healing ~ World Peace Volume I: a poetry anthology (World Healing ~ World Peace 2014) (Volume 1), Metaphor: Modern and Contemporary Poetry (Volume 1), East Coast Literary Review: Spring Edition 2014* and *Eccentric Press Poetry Anthology (Volume I): Omni Diversitas Portmanteau Volume 2(2014), 52 Loves(2015)* and *Crossing Lines Anthology(2015).*

Jose Trejo-Maya (Poetry: "System of a Down") is originally from the small rural pueblo of Tarimoro in the lowlands of Mexico (born in Celaya, Guanajuato.) After migrating to the United States in 1988 he completed his studies with an AA in Social and Behavioral Science from Citrus College, a BA in Sociology & Social Work from California State Polytechnic University, Pomona and an MFA in Creative Writing from Antioch University, Los Angeles with an emphasis in enthnopoetic language poetry of particular interest in the ancient poet

Netzahualcoyotl. He has had poems published in the *Nimrod International Journal* and *Belleville Park Pages* with several pending works.

Changming Yuan (Two Poems) is an 8-time Pushcart nominee and author of 4 chapbooks (including *Mindscaping* [2014]), and is the world's most widely published poetry author who speaks Chinese but writes English. Tutoring and co-editing *Poetry Pacific* with Allen Qing Yuan in Vancouver, Changming has poetry appearing in *Best Canadian Poetry, BestNewPoemsOnline, Cincinnati Review, Threepenny Review* and 969 other literary publications across 31 countries.

Poetry

Three Poems by Michael Mark

The Regular

Before he's two steps into the place
the counter crew sings out his name,

their voices carrying back over the line of
indistinguishables, of which I am one.

The barista stops the order he's working on to
begin his, while he takes over his part of the world.

At home, frequency gets him a shrug
of indifference and two wags from his friend's tail,

even as he places his respectable paycheck on the
kitchen table and kneels to scratch a favorite spot.

Here, others must be patient while he is served
with a complimentary cookie and squeeze of the shoulder.

As he surveys his kingdom he notices me looking
at him under the Latte-A-Thon poster,

his legs stretched over the extra chair he's
co-opted from another table.

He acknowledges he is being recognized with a bored,
royal nod then turns his attention to the subject at hand,

to rule whether the hazelnut macchiato is hot and foamy enough
and if the cookie is a sufficient offering.

He bites guardedly and considers wrapping half for someone
at home with whom he would like to curry favor.

#HappyFountainBoy

All the little fella wanted was
to splash in the fountain.

He deserved to,
for having to wear that
"Poops, I did it again" shirt.

I judged the mother as selfish
for holding him back
by his belt loop, his arms,
his neck.

What joy he would have brought
the shoppers and peppy
mall walkers.

Everyone would take out their phones,
and instantly he'd trend on twitter.
#happyfountainboy

But Reggie, or, as his mother kept
calling him,
 "No Reggie No,"
was not allowed in the fountain.

She pointed to the sign,
Entering the fountain is not permitted,
and explained, "The
policeman will take you away to jail –
and you will never see mommy again."

He listened, then broke free again,
climbing the short wall
before she brought him down, hard.

No Reggie No was a warrior! Willing
to sacrifice what was most dear for his dream!

In church, you're taught there is a God.
In nursery school, you learn conformity is success.
In the mall, the lesson is that the world hates kids.

Stores filled with stuff you can't touch,
endless waiting while parents *ooh*
and *aah* but not over you; forced
still, arms up,
while shirts are pulled off, put on
and on and on.

But then, in the middle of this hell, is a *fountain*!

Rainbow colored lights,
pennies and dimes sparkling,
warping under the water.

But you are not allowed in!
No, No Reggie No, you
cannot get soaked and dance to the
mall music, make clappy hands,
find treasures for mommy, splash her.

So, out of solidarity and boredom,
as my wife was still in the stores,
*ooh*ing and *aah*ing over something
other than me,
I began to untie my shoelaces.

And wondered where I could buy
a "Wild Thing" shirt.

I'd pick up two.

Fresh Air

Drape your arm
around my neck,
I feel your five year old hand
reaching for your father's.

Put your head
in my lap,
I hear your infant cries for
your mother's milk.

Hook your finger
around my belt loop, and
tug me to your side
I feel you in the womb
refusing to leave.

Say you can't help
but be possessive of me
because you love me more than
your own breath,
I feel your pillow pressed over my face.

Threaten I would be no one
without you,
I feel the fresh air
from a cracked window
in an apartment
that has no number or letter or name
on the door.

Short Story

Need
By Robin Wyatt Dunn

No one I knew I knew before I held you. No one I knew I knew before I knew who you were, when I saw you by the pool, by my motel room.

I wish I could have done more than I did; I love you still.

It's twisted but it's enough; this was my life.

And no one can say I knew something that I didn't, that I had some inkling of our coming story, over the American roads.

They're mine but they're dying, so just let me tell you about this before they're dead, before I am.

Her name was Annabelle Exquisite Surf, she of two mothers, two lesbians from Fruitvale.

I was ready to check out (from life, not the motel) but then I saw her, and thought, well, you know what I thought.

Just look at that body.

And: maybe not yet.

I wish it could have been different but this is what it is, a small moral tragedy, of the sort you read about in books. Or ought to read about, before they snuff it out.

Are you ready?

1. What Weezer Says

It's a starry night that it begins on, two nights after I seduced young Annabelle and took her promptly from her Arizona motel room, sans parents, sans everything but her hoodie and her fine down jacket. And her purse, and a change of clothes.

This starry night it's mine, still now, as the land is mine, as the man says, this land is my land, this land is your land, from Staten island, to the new york highlands. Now I know where Staten Island is at, that's the landfill one, but I don't know where those highlands are at. Maybe he means those monk towers over the Palisades, where the Jesuits roosted like Crows in the long ago. Or maybe that's upstate somewhere in the Adirondacks, in armed territory.

Some starry nights are better than others. Some fall in lockstep with you, and never let you go. No matter how much you might want them to.

"Pass me the pipe, honey," she said, and I did.

Her ass was the sort of fruit not every tree grows, like one of those superfruits they try to market from time to time, the fruit of the Amazon come now available through technology, and modern political dynamics—

Her eyes were less desirable, if only more lonely, but they contained too why I am telling this story, their need. Need is related to the word death, related to the word corpse. It's hard to write about need. We want to hear about the land of plenty, the land of milk and honey.

But what *this land is your land, this land is my land* leaves out, is that this is a land of need.

We got enough weed for now but what we don't have is time; it's running out . . .

"Drive faster, honey," she said. And I did, as she inhaled the smegma aroma of lost American centuries, wisdom that will not be counted. Who I am, lost over my need—

***

And last at right this dike over my oils and ills, this droomy dream bow I sail on slow, like YoYoMa's bow, over her body, ode on a G string, unto her G spot, on my last night, before who I was soon to become, her man—

She was moaning hot on the grass. The serpent and the fable, and I'll be done before I'm able, to reaffirm—

***

It's like Weezer says: *oh yea. all right.*

But not yet, not enough. I owe you a little more than that. My government-to-be. My not-quite-there confessor.

This is a jukebox, then, imagine me with my cheap mike and my drool-boy curls:

6

I was a man with a plaaaaaan!
One that didn't work out.
Being an artist by nature, though one with but few works to his name, I
considered suicide, and bought a gun.
And put it in my mouth.
And pulled the trigger.
I blew my brains out!
Only not really . . .

What happened was the bullet struck my two front teeth and ricocheted straight out, taking my teeth with them.

Mom and Dad had to pay for the replacements (and I had to get out of there before the cops showed up).

So like Weezer says: *like father. Stepfather. The son is drowning in the flood—*

And that's me, or close enough. Drowning in my petite American flood, my petite American flood of Annabelle and the last century where we can pretend to mean shit . . . my heart is yours, I promise you that much, whatever happens—

***

"What're you doin?" she asked, sitting there in her bikini, dangling a leg in the water.

"Workin' hard or hardly workin,'" I said.

"What do you do," she said.

"I depose small governments with the stroke of my pen," I told her. And she smiled, just a little.

I don't know what she was smiling at. Maybe it was just my clothes. I hadn't changed them in five days.

"Where are your parents?" I said.

"At Costco," she said.

"You want to run away with me?" I asked her.

"All right," she said. "Just let me get my stuff

2. The Jerusalem Room

You can play there for days in the desert and no one will kick you out, as long as you have money to pay the keeper, and songs to sing.

I can sing forever, though my voice isn't that good, and my songs are other men's.

The Jerusalem Room is one of those pieces of paradise you can still find in America, where no one knows your name, and no one cares to, where you can drink whiskey like water and watch the sun rise over the sky like a nuclear daydream, hotter than my love, or yours, hotter than fuel, hotter than my fear under the sentence I now face (a terrorism charge), hotter than one kilo of C4, hotter than my heart, and its twisted avenues of maintenance. The desert around The Jerusalem Room in Death Valley, California is a joy.

"Dance with me!" Annabelle said, and I did, sipping the last of the whiskey.

The Jerusalem Room's monetary habits are part of a growing American trend: you pay to play the piano in The Jerusalem Room. Just like every rock and roll star you've heard of in the last thirty years was the son or daughter of a rich rock and roll star.

I get the monthly deposits in my account and I don't bug my parents, except when I shoot my teeth out, and in return I get to partake in the American tragedy, of a man at the piano, who does not ask for change, who does not solicit songs, or take requests, because he can do just about whatever he wants at that keyboard and folks will listen, as long as he buys the drinks.

As long as the mood stays quiet and ridiculous. Like the end of the world.

"Dance faster!" she says, pouting, and I do, already a little drunk, watching her ass swing in the morning desert breeze.

If a woman can do anything, it's not make you go sane, but something that can be called a cousin to sanity, which is purpose. And you can choose a sane or an insane purpose, but women appreciate a purposeful man, even if his purpose be self-destruction.

I no longer do drugs. But I don't mind if you do them. That's fine with me.

The Jerusalem Room is my sanity. With the insane colors of the ruins glued all over the walls, like an exploded Hollywood dressing room. With the chintz and the glints of flint you'll notice from the barkeep and owner Mr. John, a face you'll soon never see again, as he is set to depart our American Story, with pancreatic cancer.

"Go break my last C-note and get me a bottle of whiskey," I said to Annabelle, striking up some Edward Elgar.

Elgar's no tight ass even though he was a Brit. He's delirious. Exquisite. Rich mellifluous and rigid, not like a square, but like an arrow, made by the finest fletcher of the city, fired straight for your besieging heart—

If I need Elgar I need you, deeper than anything, deeper than this time now, so young and already so broken, deeper than this problem I've developed lately, of remembering how who I'm supposed to be in the near future doesn't jive with who I've recently become . . .

An asshole with a very cute jailbait high-schooler on his arm. Drinking booze illegal for her mouth. Smoking dope (provided by her, admittedly), similarly *verboten*, as she lacks a medical license.

I insisted she go on the pill as I've never been very good with condoms and so dragged her to a Planned Parenthood clinic in Barstow, for, while I'm sure she'd make a reasonably good mother, the evidence of my crime would then be inescapable.

But I suppose I've already broken federal law in transporting a minor female across state lines for immoral purposes.

My defense then rests, your honor, on the morality of my purpose.

The Jerusalem Room is called the Jerusalem Room because an old and crazy Jew bought the place in the mid 1950s and proceeded to glue the cultural effluvia which now make the place famous all over its walls.

Perhaps, some day, I too can be an old and crazy Jew. If I ever get out of California . . .

"Let me pour it for you, honey," she said, and I smelled her hair mixed with the Jack Daniel's as I played Elgar's dog running for the bone, down the piano . . .

3. Dinosaurs

While I drive I take my front teeth out with my lower lip, making them stick out at a 90 degree angle, then I pop them back in, and she laughs.

She laughs when I play the giraffe. I make a good giraffe (down in my heart), holding the wheel like a tree, and looking for leaves on the road. The giraffe is solid. Tall. Serious. Elegant (well I'm not that). Refined. The giraffe is an interloper who does not interlope. He overlopes. He steps right over the problem, to his food.

I wish I could do that.

My problem is the woman in the car with me. It's not even for the sex I love her, but for her eyes. She's even more lonely than I am.

"Where do you want to go, honey?" I ask her.

"Madagascar!" she shouts.

"Where that I can drive you to?"

"I want to see dinosaurs!" she shouts.

Dinosaurs I can do.

***

Are you listening? Am I getting through? *Hey, what station is this—*

***

We heard gunshots that night. Not the last ones I would hear, unfortunately.

But that was later and this is now, heading into a kind of sleep, though I'm still driving the car, heading east, toward the dark horizon, watching the stars come out, slipping my hand between her legs, and she's still awake, but her eyes are closed.

I cup her sex, some mercurial salvation, a big ticket item in a stripped down Communist-era market. I hold her sex with my right hand and the wheel with my left and the highway is eternal, and so am I.

***

What I found out later (but should have figured out sooner) was that this was not the first time my little angel had done this. Run off with a man without a word. So I was fortunate, as it turned out, that I was not the first Romeo to traipse up her virginal bower, because her two mothers back at that motel in Arizona did not at once notify the authorities. They knew she'd be back.

But she was far wiser than me, and what a man doesn't ask he has no right to know, and so all I knew was that she loved me (she'd told me that right away).

The night was too big for words.

***

"What are you doing?" she said to me, standing outside our motel room, that second night.

"I don't know."

"What do you want to be doing?" she said.

"You," I said.

"No, really."

"I don't know."

"Me either," she said. "Let's go to sleep. Tomorrow it's dinosaurs!"

***

I am not anyone. No one in particular.

She is someone. I do not know who she is.

I belong nowhere, and everywhere, which means I can be anyone. Whereas she knows ...

"Are we out of weed?" she asks sleepily from the motel bed.

"Yes."

"Fuck . . ."

She knows who she needs to be. Her body is more useful than mine is. She is Protean. Assertive. She needs more marijuana.

"I don't get paid till next week."

"That's okay," she says.

I sit down by her warm body and look at the desert sunlight through the thin curtain.

I have to take her back to Los Angeles. I have to never return to Los Angeles.

"It's dinosaurs today," I say.

"Oh yeah!" Her small, round face is delicious in joy. I give her a kiss, then scoop her nude body from out of the bed and dress her, while she giggles. Something is happening but I do not know what it is. Love, I suppose, but I don't recognize what kind ...

If I am careful. If I live my life without too many buzzwords. If I live at a sufficient distance from the wrong sorts of people. If I remember to remain productive. And useful. Warm. If I am borne on you—borne by you—and I bear you back ...

If I am careful I will be allowed to keep her. As a prize. As appreciation. This is what I tell myself. It is too much, but it was what I told myself.

She hopped in to the car and I drove north, throwing the motel key at the window of the clerk, who raised his fist in comic rage, towards dinosaurs:

She is not my appendage. She is my extrusion. She is not my property. She is my prison guard.

"Baby you're beautiful," I say.

She snorts with laughter.

"Pull over I want to suck on your cock," she says.

"Safety first," I say, pulling over.

The horizon comes from the word *horos*, boundary. The boundary is the most beautiful thing. It can not be described in words. It is only barely felt in the medulla. The boundary is God.

I hold tighter onto the steering wheel.

***

We beg a joint from the proprietor of Dinosaur Haven, a huge and good-natured aging hippy, with a braided beard and a small huge-eyed dog who looks stoned.

I don't get high any more; really I don't. But I got high with her.

The *Stegosaurus*, I realize, inhaling carefully, is a fruiting body. The *Stegosaurus* is a cosmic flower, seeking starlight, and pollen, with its long lows in the jungle dark.

"Catch me!" she cries and runs between the *Pleiosaurs* and *Triceratops*, their large bodies anchored with rusted metal bolts to the desert earth. They stand over me like the gates of Uruk. She is my Enkidu, though not my servant, though I am perhaps more wild than she. Together we can slay Humbaba, if she will reveal her evil face, if I can stand to face danger for Annabelle, if I can knock her up—

I pass her the joint underneath the *Brontosaur* and lean back against the polished fiberglass body. Doesn't anybody love dinosaurs anymore?

They do, I know. Though we are the only ones here. The only ones who could afford the gasoline today.

If we are in the Middle Ages I am a reluctant nobleman, of middling bloodlines and no particular talents. Perhaps above-average health for a noble, having taken up scribbling in lieu of drugs.

"What's that one?" she asks.

"*Archaeopteryx.*"

"It looks like a bird."

"It's a dinosaur bird."

"I want a pet *Archaeopteryx*," she says.

"I'll get you one. But call your parents first. So they don't worry."

"I'll send them a text."

"Okay."

She types out her message.

"What did you say?" I ask.

"I said 'Met a fun guy!' "

I laugh. "Well good," I say.

A *Pterodactyl* has a certain headiness about it, notwithstanding its huge and pointed head, its musicality of form can be understood as a moral lesson for the human species: of who we could be, if only we want it bad enough—

I want her bad enough but what I want about her is something I cannot have, her energy, and her innocence, her particular fragrance, as of a morning in some French peasant village of oak and disaster—

Tell me who you will become and I will tell you my name, it's Travis the Traveler, and I will be for you what you could be for me, if only you want it bad enough; your voice.

Let me be your voice, as Ian Holm in that terrible dead school bus movie is the voice for the grieving parents, let me speak for your suffering, so that I can be saved—

4. Fruitvale

"Where were you going with your parents?" I ask, driving.

"Home."

"Where had you been?"

"Texas."

"How come you're not a Lesbian like your moms?"

"Maybe I will be."

"I'm just kidding."

"I'm not."

***

That day was our first encounter with the police.

***

I dreamt of the dinosaurs that night. I was a dinosaur, or a kind of dinosaur. My territory moved over me and under me, lifting me up, and filling me. My mate was over the escarpment, moaning, her voice like a river from a previous era, filled overbrimming with messages only a few of which I was able to decode.

I'm hungry . . .
and
I'm in love.
I awoke in sweat. She was staring at me, standing in the room.
"What is it?" I said.
"I have to leave."
"Okay."

***

My money has amusing legal entanglements associated with it. I receive approximately $800 per month from my trust fund. Unlike other trust fund babies, however, the full sum of my estate will never enter into my hands.

My deceased uncle, who deemed me his peculiar beneficiary, decided to donate the entirety of my inheritance to the Republican Party upon my death.

Thus, while I am assured respite from starvation and homelessness, I must also work the system diligently to cover my basic needs, such as health insurance, which I finally managed to achieve from Medi-Cal, the coverage for the poor. But many other forms of governmental relief I do not qualify for, since I am, technically, independently wealthy.

Of course, I could always go to work. But no employer seems to value the skills I have.

Even my car will soon grow unaffordable. Then I will be unable to leave Los Angeles.

***

The encounter with the police had shaken both of us, I knew. I didn't want to let on that it had. We both were gloomy now.

Throw off society, this is easy to do. But society will never throw you off. You are one of us.

I had had my license and registration. No outstanding warrants. But drivers are few and far between these days. And Annabelle's lack of identification had not pleased the officer.

California law hung over us both like a grim smog.

I was driving her to Fruitvale. Her mothers were expecting us.

***

As a suicidal, recovering addict I could hardly claim to be an attractive mate for Annabelle, but Mrs. and Mrs. Exquisite Surf Wordsworth did not immediately throw me out their door, or greet me with a shotgun.

"Hello," said Mrs. Wordsworth, standing on her high porch. The two women almost looked like twins, though they were three inches different in height. Both graying, both serious looking.

"Mom, mom, this is Travis," said Annabelle, standing halfway up the porch steps, between me and the mothers.

"Won't you come in Travis," said Mrs. Wordsworth.

We'd driven all day and it was starting to catch up with me. But I would not faint and ruin the show.

"Annabelle tells us you're a filmmaker," said Mrs. Wordsworth, gesturing towards an armchair.

"Former," I said, seating myself on the edge of the large chair. In the lions' den.

"It's nice of you to bring our Annabelle back to us," said the other Mrs. Wordsworth, watching me with cool eyes.

"The least I can do," I said.

"Yes," said Mrs. Wordsworth. "I'm sorry, we haven't introduced ourselves. I'm Kathy, this is Margaret. Maggie, won't you get us some tea?"

"Do you take green tea?" asked Margaret.

"Sure," I said. "Thank you."

Annabelle hovered behind my chair, watching her mothers. She seemed pleased with herself. She'd brought home fresh meat for dinner . . .

"Thank you for not calling the police," I found myself saying.

"Why would we do that?" asked Kathy, smiling.

"Well, thank you for not doing it," I said.

"What do you do these days then, Travis?"

"I'm between jobs, Mrs. Wordsworth."

"Kathy please."

We sat in silence, except for Annabelle, who remained standing. I drank my green tea.

"He's taking me to Hollywood," said Annabelle. This was news to me.

Kathy's eyes widened. "Oh?" she said.

"I'm going to be a famous actress."

Both mothers laughed. I smiled nervously. Say something, Travis.

"She really is a remarkable young woman," I said.

"Yes," said Kathy, standing and putting her arm around her daughter for the first time since we'd come in. "Yes she is."

The mothers regarded their offspring. Who was the father? I hadn't asked.

"You'll sleep in the living room, Travis," said Margaret. "There's a futon."

"Sure," I said.

***

The morning light hurt my eyes.

"We're going shopping," said Kathy. "Our daughter is going to need new clothes for her big debut."

"What?' I said, regarding my new prospective-mother-in-law from beneath the thin white sheet.

"In Hollywood. If you need us, the number is on the kitchen table."

Annabelle waved goodbye.

I lay in the futon in the Bay Area morning light.

It was warm, like a lot of Bay Area homes; inviting. It reminded me of England in some ways, these homes, little nooks and crannies, granola and clean living.

I found my way to the shower and saw the white bucket in the stall. SAVE WATER the bucket announced.

I turned on the shower, letting it warm up, listening to the pitter patter into the bucket.

Lesbian mothers were very strong, I realized. The gay community in Hollywood would be strong allies, I realized . . . but somewhat overbearing . . .

What was I thinking. Did I really intend to abscond with the young woman? But I'd already absconded with her. The women were merely calling my bluff.

I was trapped.

I stepped into the hot stream of water and tried to forget that I was a man.

5. Hollywood

I am a failure as a human being, but this is all right. I fail very well indeed.

***

Hollywood is a great light and we moths move towards it. Not all moths see the light, but those who do move towards it.

Some are eaten, swallowed by the light . . . killed.

Some live in its embrace, dying slowly. Living richly.

In the darkness that surrounds the light, the moths can discern the outlines of the landscape. Here, a porch. Here, a rocking chair. There, the porch swing. Above, the night.

The Hollywood light is a powerful radiation. The weirdos come here because, even if you weren't weird when you arrive, the radiation will mutate you.

This is why moths seek the light, despite its killing force. It gives knowledge.

It gives power.

The great light of Hollywood is both death and religion. What else can it be, for little moths?

***

I am no exception. I swirl too around its light. But I am fortunate in that I have seen it kill people and know it now for what it is. It almost killed me too. So I decided to make my home near the light, and never go too close to it.

Even that is dangerous. It will likely try to kill me again. But I do not want to leave it.

It is like no place else.

***

"Oh my god I'm in Hollywood!" said Annabelle, in her jean shorts and hat and sunglasses. I wore my traditional black.

I was now her manager.

"Yes, you're in Hollywood."

"Oh my God, where are the movie stars?"

"They're in the hills, honey, and in Malibu, hiding away."

"Aww."

"But we can see the stars on the sidewalk."

We moved through the gentle crowd, reading some of the names under our feet. We stopped and had our photo taken with Marilyn Monroe, who sits so kindly by the subway, her skirt blowing up forever. They always find a good look-a-like; they capture her spirit, whatever the shape of the nose, or the exact length and shade of her hair.

***

I suppose I'm not a failure as a human being. I'm not a eunuch. I'm not Adolph Hitler. I don't murder people for a living. I don't train and manipulate child soldiers. I just commit statutory rape.

The statute is like a statue, like David, larger than life. But I am smaller than David, and less eternal. I may die any day now.

"I want a hot dog!" she cried.

"And you shall have one."

We eat the dogs under the nuclear sunlight, not knowing what horror is. Almost unable to imagine it.

She is talented, I know that much. The question is, how shall I use her talent. Talent is something that wants to be used; it wants harnessing. I must use her delicately, and well. But even this assumes I will be able to get the modest permits. But that is easy enough; no, what I am assuming is that she will want me to direct her.

"So you want to be in the movies, dollface?"

"Yeah." She smiles at me.

"You're here at the right age."

"Lucky me!"

18

"We'll have to get us a Backstage, see what's new."

"Not today though. Tomorrow."

"All right. Tomorrow."

She is afraid. So am I.

"What kind of part do you want?" I ask her.

Around us we can see some aspiring actors already, a couple of them clutching headshots and resumes. A few more wait outside the photo studio, practicing the fine art of patience. In the distance, a pimp dressed in bright yellow including a huge top hat swivels his ass and plays with his cane.

"Look at that pimp! Oh my god," says Annabelle.

"He is definitely a pimp."

"I want a good part," Annabelle says. "A really good part."

"Yes, those are the hard ones to find."

"We'll find one," she says. She presses her lips together.

"Meanwhile I'll write you a good one."

"Yes, do that!"

She runs in to a clothing shop and I follow her around, enjoying the attention a pretty girl gets you.

"I'm sending moms a pic!"

"Very good."

She stands on the streetcorner, and takes her selfie, one arm wrenched around my neck, the other extended above, holding her phone.

In the shot, she grins like a mannequin doll, imperturbable, and I am the growling behemoth shuffling in her bright wake, the entourage.

The hanger on.

"I'm your hanger-on," I say, looking at the photo on her bright pink phone.

"Yes," she says, and kisses me on the cheek.

Poetry

Food for Thought by Ndaba Sibanda

Food For Thought

to swig because
something is given
is to tempt and test
the patience of such
comrades as Sir Vomit
or Constipation too far
like a silly bare tongue
kissing Ms. Electricity

to dance to the tune
of a sick fire is only musical
when the extinguishers
and firemen are working

to make a series of turnarounds
till one is really dizzy and does
not know where and how to stop
is to have an upside-down dream
whose closest relative is Nightmare

Poetry

Three Poems by Alex Hughes

Beautiful are Turtles and Snails

Beautiful are turtles and snails and other
Be-shelled animals; descend the secret
Nautilus. Compressed odors grow stale
In the inner smoking-room; rotting colors
Hide in darkened corners; weakness strides
In strength beneath that sheltering dome,
A child imprisoned thinking prison's home—
And ever on they forward move, behind
That shell and shield, till death's power
Stabs or the secret terror yields—

Inscrutable and beautiful.

The Curse of Peace

Many an evening I wonder whether
Past blessings are atonement for
Future wrongs. A golden youth
Reaches spider legs through time
To spin a web of fear and longing:
At best, I know, I'll maintain the status
Quo, and at worst—oh, and worse!
The whole world spins beneath that
Dangling web. The silken tendrils
Quiver at the shiver running through
My hand—then snap! The Fall waits
Before all men, lurking with waiting
Blade to cut the cord. And in that
Certain plummet, I'll have time to
Ponder whether that sheltered youth
Was a blessing or a darker truth.

The Whorl of Humanity

There's a flower in the desert.
It's tilted and sun-wilted and
Rather small, but sturdy and
Hardy amid the lonely desert
Sprawl. A bird of prey screams
Over from horizon to horizon,
A beautiful terror from the devil's
Dreams, and the flower braces
Against the roaring power. One by
One its petals tumble as the
Ground begins to rumble, singing
A song of right and wrong, until
Only the hardened stalk remains
To feed anger to its desert pains.

Poetry

Folds by Darren Demaree

Folds

The man is creased, ropey
in fact, all weight

& muscle, without strength
& thus, we can give him

not a single gift
that he can keep forever.

How useless to look
like a god, to carry nothing.

Short Story

Parades
by R. A. Morean

He stands, one hip out, looking at sweating bottles of green tea through the glass of the General Store's refrigerator. He is leggy-tall and I mean stringy with legs. Slender, slight, sinewy, and at the pelvis is where the tutu flares—usually hot pink or perhaps purple with a slip of white. Today, mid-June, the wavering fan is a swirl of pastels. Adding to his height are strappy sequined heels, open toed, revealing large horny feet, chipped nails, and a ring circling each pinkie. Bangles and bracelets jangle when he walks, a hand fluttering to his chest when accosted on the street for either overly friendly gossip or expletives. No conversation ever floats in the space between.

He sighs and looks at me for help. Which would I prefer? The Ginger Parade or Pomegranate Smoothie? Bright blue dual swaths of shadow curve like monotone rainbows above each eye and red lips part quickly, too eager to smile. That smile is swift—he's learned to deflect the dichotomies he lives with, the 1's and 0's of a polarized life. He is, oddly, the physical embodiment of nuance.

I say, go for the ginger, adding how expensive the glass bottles are. He sighs and agrees and stakes a claim: beautiful things are pricey. He turns away and selects the ginger, and the silly silver spandex top fitting snug and more secure than any I could ever wear, accentuates small breasts and a flapper's waistline. He pauses and sets the bottle back on the shelf, the hand resting on this chest again, like a large stunned bird, motionless but somehow wired for instant flight.

"But ginger can be so stingy on the back of my throat," he says and reaches again, the other hand moving, this time for the purple red pomegranate.

Then a young man walks past us and thick soled biker boots leave a little rubber smear on the floor when he rounds the corner, finds us and our discussion, and momentum is scuffed. The two of us glance at him and he smiles, his skin very white and his wavy hair dyed blue-black. He has a bouquet of cheap orange carnations and a soft cantaloupe tucked under his arm like a football. His heavy leather jacket is bright with silvery spikey cones waving with every move like fat porcupine quills.

"Ooo, look at you," says my new friend. "Nice studs."

The boy does not look at him, but finds me and says proudly, "I did these myself. Took a week. Blistered up my hand."

After he leaves, the man in the tutu changes his mind. "I think I'll take the ginger anyway," he says. "Sometimes the burn is good."

"I always want to be the parade," he told me once, brushing back a strand of blond wig-hair with one large, flat, manicured hand.

But I know a parade of one is lonely.

Vol. 6, No. 3

Poetry

System of a Down by Jose Trejo-Maya

System of a Down

I
still
hear the
voices of
the Lakota
Ghost Dancers
       fateful
       journey
       Sioux–Oglala:
              mourning
              the system
              is down or
              look on the periphery.
                       Postscript:
                          To perceives
                          not to go back
                          to the past these
                          are fine prints to
                          remind you we are
                          All brethren and one.
                                  I write because I can,
                                  others are _____.
                                  It's a mixed bag there's
                                  an old Arabian proverb:
                                  I thank you for your Life.

I
say
what
needs
to be said
not what most
want to hear:_____.
_____ some
one is missing something somewhere.
To the *Inipi*/Sweatlodge Ceremony will
revive the lost story. I still remember—these words

Brother you are an Aztec you do not need no passport.
This more than a reference point I too don't condone ignorance with rapport:
Panquetzaliztli Macuil –Acatl Chicueyi Acatl [Gregorian Calendar: December 29, 1890]

Short Story

Family Honor
By Frank Pray

The dome of the Temple Mount beamed golden as the morning sun awakened Jerusalem. This morning, as so many others, Jacob parted the living room curtains to search for the white bearded figure with his long coat and dark wide-brimmed hat. Seeing his grandfather, he would whiz out the front door to where the old man would kneel on the street with open arms to catch the boy. Jacob nuzzled his face into the old man's beard, delighted at how the soft hairs tickled his nose.

"I won't let you go until you make me sneeze," the boy would say, and the old man, as he did every morning grabbed in the air for imaginary sneezes. "Get away from my Jacob," the old man warned the daemons. The boy, often pretending, would sneeze, and the old man would mourn or feign great anger: "One got away grandpa!" Jacob squealed as if they had not done this dozens of times before.

On their final morning together, Jacob pulled his grandfather toward the jacaranda tree, its carpet marking the warm scent of pastries on display at Moshen's. The boy's mouth watered as he imagined the green, blue, and orange icings. He skipped as the heat of the sidewalk pushed through his sandals. A hummingbird hovered over them. Jacob pointed to the green and ruby whir of the zigzagging spectacle. "He sparkles, Grandpa." The tiny tinctured thing thrust towards them. Jacob spun to the bird's antics. "David's dance," the old man laughed.

His grandfather walked faster at the boy's lead. When they reached the blossomed ground, a tall hooded figure wearing the black and white keffiyeh stepped from a nearby car. His grandfather pushed Jacob hard as the stranger took several steps, and lifted his Caracal semiautomatic. The boy rolled onto the ground as the roar of gunfire and shattered glass filled the morning air. Rivulets of red pushed against the fallen petals. Bits of red and gray splattered the icings.

***

For months after the assassination, Jacob did not speak. Miriam, his mother, held him through the night, often awakened by the twitching and cold sweat of his body.

When the boy's trembling subsided, Miriam would quietly return to her bed. Some months later, the boy did not ask for his mother again. He regained his voice, but his words were few. Not once did he mention that day with his grandfather.

In the same year his grandfather died, Jacob began the traditional study of the Talmud at the Jewish day school near East Jerusalem.

***

At age 16, Jacob began yeshiva, the time of study with the local Hasidic rabbi.

"Rabbi, why do other nations not accept that Jerusalem belongs only to us?" "Child, we are people of the Book. Study His Word, and you will see Elohim gave the Land of Israel to the Jews. We are Adonai's protected ones. No mere man can dispute this.

"Tell me, why is the Holy City ours alone?" the rabbi entoned.

"Because Jerusalem is our eternal capital. It must not be parceled by men," Jacob echoed. But daily, as he grew into manhood, Jacob saw the truth of Israel's divisions everywhere. The walls of the old city and the Temple Mount, were in the Palestinian sector. 135 miles of fencing stretching from Gaza to Jerusalem separated "them" from "us." The fence, like a growth chart his grandfather kept at his bedroom door marked a decade of Jacob's life from age six to sixteen.

***

In his sixteenth year, Jacob enrolled in the military academy, wearing his uniform even on days when it was not required. One day, the local *rasan*, an executive officer who limped, toured the Academy with a *brigadier-general* looking for recruits.

"Who is that boy?" the brigadier asked.

"Cadet Jacob Moskovitz, sir."

The two old soldiers watched Jacob doing his drills. The brigadier's trained eye followed the sharp turns and sudden spins as the young cadet moved his weapon with textbook perfection.

"Who taught him to do that?"

"He teaches himself sir. He's here everyday, watching, asking questions."

The brigadier walked over to Jacob, who stood to attention, and executed a sharp salute.

"At ease cadet," the brigadier said. "Son, your discipline puts our regulars to shame."

"That's not my goal, *tat aluf.*"

"What is you goal, cadet?"

"Israel."

"You have the makings of a soldier, Cadet Moskovitz."

"Thank you sir,"

"Would you like to train with the men?"

"Sir, more than anything, sir."

"I'll arrange it," the brigadier said.

At eighteen, Jacob applied for officer training while his schoolmates applied for extended yeshiva to avoid conscription. On his way to guard duty one day, he encountered an old schoolmate walking to class. Jacob returned his friend's excited recognition with a cold nod. These cowards used yeshiva not to find the truth, but to hide from it.

Cadet Moskovitz quickly impressed his superiors. His cadet commander assigned him to a checkpoint at the East sector to examine Palestinian identification cards. He questioned each person, probing for reasons to have him or her expelled from the City.

One evening after duty Jacob opened the door to his mother's house to the aroma of sambousak pie and vegetable gratin. He imagined his grandfather sitting at the end of the dinner table, as his mother laid out the plates of rice and bulgar pilafs, with, shwarma, falafel or hummus. His grandfather would pronounce the Kiddush on Friday evening, between the time of the setting sun and the appearance of the first three stars in the night sky. Jacob would wait in the garden. With each new star, he jumped into his grandfather's lap. "I saw the third one Grandpa. Now say the blessing!" On this night, two decades later, it was Jacob who said the Kiddush, repeating the scriptures exactly as his grandfather did.

As they ate, he told his mother he had signed on for six years in the Special Forces.

"Why did you do this?" his mother asked.

"To honor our family."

"Has violence worked for us?"

"Sometimes we have no choice."

"And sometimes we act as if killing is the only choice."

"I'm joining."

"Why not defer, like the other men?"

"I'm needed now."

When she saw he would not relent, her voice softened. "You mustn't die."

"I won't die."

Frustrated, she asked again, "Why did you do this?"

"Grandfather." His voice was faint as if whispered in a dream.

"Grandfather? Grandfather died working for peace."

Not knowing what to say, he shot back, "You dishonor him."

His words pressed against her like spikes, leaving her breathless.

Why did she think she honored grandfather? Why did she light her memorial candle at his picture each year? Twenty four times he watched its tendril of smoke weave a refrain to his impotence as his grandfather's face moved in and out of the shadows.

"Grandfather was a warrior, and prepared to die," he told his still-silent mother.

"He loved peace. He wanted an end to this," she said.

"There can be no end until they are crushed."

"They?"

"The Palestinians."

"All of them?"

"Every one of them." His voice turned shrill and his words shot like bullets in her direction.

"Your neighbors? The people you work with?"

She walked to him, as if he were still a boy, and placed her hands on his shoulders. He was nearly a foot taller than she.

"Here is the enemy," she said, placing her palm against his chest.

He pulled away, and left quickly for the military compound. His mother's talk was crazy. Had she lost sight of the dangers? The enemy would never go away. He knew force was the only answer.

He finally relaxed as he drove past the guard gate into the compound. He felt most at home here, away from his mother's misguided softness. Had she forgotten how grandfather died because of such wishful thinking?

***

The old man had joined a peace group whose motto was 'One people, One peace." Together the neighbors formed a committee covering ten blocks of Jerusalem. Five Israelis and five Palestinians crossed invisible barriers to draft a peace manifesto, citing from both the Koran and the Torah. The ten signed on behalf of 30,000 in the city.

The manifesto irritated both Likud and the PLO. Agreeing on nothing else, the old enemies discovered a common goal in discrediting the Committee's hold on the world's imagination.

***

For over a decade, Jacab chased his dream of promotion. The brigadier-general who first saw promise in the boy years earlier appointed him to command a Special Forces unit. When Miriam returned from her son's installation, she retreated to the deep cushions of her father's old worn chair to read from the prophet Isaiah. She loved the way the old chair cradled her in its massive padded arms. In it, she separated from her fears. She was fifty-five, her father's age when he was killed. Sitting in his chair all these years later, she heard the cooing of morning doves in the garden, and prayed for her son's safety. She did this every day, as if the trees were minarets, and the doves were the Muezzin.

Late in the afternoon, she listened to news reports of angry young Palestinians gathering in the streets only a few blocks away. She turned off the reports. Still, she heard the faint sounds of protest, and police sirens through her garden window. The phone rang. It was Rosha, her childhood friend, asking her to join several other women to make a statement of peace to the protestors . Miriam was tired, but to honor her father's memory, she joined her old friends.

Why do you do this? Jacob argued with his mother over the years. No one listens to you.. And it was true. She knew it was true. She knew it was true each time an Israeli or Palestinian sneered at her, or crushed a pamphlet in his fist, making sure she saw him toss it away.

Miriam gathered at Rosha's house with their friends. The women had shared passages from bride, to mother, to grandmother. Holding only their signs as weapons, the five women looked at one another for a moment, without speaking. Miriam patted a shoulder, grasped a hand, straightened a collar, or smiled an encouragement. Then they began to walk toward the frenzied shouting.

Their few signs for peace were met by hundreds of other signs moving down the street like steaming lava. "Death to the Zionists," "Exterminate the Jews," "Israel kills Palestinian children," "Israel killed my father," "Death to the Invaders," "Death to the Zionists," "Death to America."

"Go home you old fools," one the youths screamed. "Get out of here!" another young man ordered, his voice and eyes wild at seeing troops gathering in battle position at the end of the street.

A protestor, his eyes red from tear gas, his clothing smeared with sweat and grime, accused the women of being Israeli stooges.

The demonstrators spat and yelled as they passed Miriam. "Zionist whores." "Liars." "Murderers."

A bare chested man with a red and white-checkered scarf across his face pushed her hard, causing her to fall. Then he turned to join the others in the crowd yelling threats and throwing rocks at the soldiers who stood with shields behind a barricade. Someone in the crowd fired shots into the advancing phalanx of soldiers.

In the melee, Miriam tried to run, but she could only hobble. "Save us Adonai," she prayed, but the words turned to stone in her mouth as she watched a rip of bullets spread across the mass of people jammed into the street. A swath of Palestinian men collapsed as if an invisible knife had sliced through the crowd.

On Company Commander Moskovitz's order, a second gunner opened fire from the opposite side of the street. The crazed men around Miriam shoved or pulled her out of the way. She saw the head of a man explode just in front of her, his brains like curdled milk spotting her face. Something like a steel rod thrust into her back, slamming her into her into the arms of one of the protestors. "Why are you looking at me that way?" she wanted to ask the young man, who held her for a few seconds, staring at her. His sweet frightened face reminded her of Jacob's so many years ago when she cradled him against the nightmares. She looked down to see a circle of blood at the center of her chest spread like an enlarging eye until it covered her breasts. In the last seconds of consciousness, she heard Jacob's voice as he yelled orders to his men. Jacob smiled to see the entangled legs and arms, then turned grim to hide his jackaled joy.

The news the next day reported there were five Israeli women inexplicably mixed into the crowd. When Commander Jacob Moskovitz saw his mother's name on the list of dead, he insisted there was a mistake. He knew that going to the morgue, he would confirm the mistake. But when he pulled the sheet from the body to see his mother's blood drained face, a roar rose in his chest, filling the room until it ended with a rhythmic moaning. Several of his men, standing outside rushed into the room to see their *seren* curled on the floor, gasping for air. For the second time in his life, he could not speak.

During the days of mourning, his *sgan aluf*, the lieutenant-colonel, told him. "Call the rabbi. It is disrespectful to delay the funeral." When Jacob did not answer, the commander ordered one of his men to fetch the rabbi, and designated two of his lieutenants to act as "Shomers," the traditional watchmen who stay with the body until the burial.

"We need to call the Chevra Kadisha for the ritual of purification," one of his mother's friends whispered in Jacob's ear as he sat staring into his mother's garden. He turned towards the woman, his face muted and void. When he did not answer, she patted him on the arm. "I will see that they are called," she whispered again.

On the day of the funeral, Jacob dressed in his formal military uniform. He looked at the black ribbon one of the women had given him, then threw it aside. He went to his mother's sewing kit, found the scissors, and cut a wide tear across the left side of his coat. He remembered the day his mother explained the custom when his grandfather died. "When a parent dies, the child is to wear a black ribbon or cut a tear in his clothing on the left side, to show the tear between life and death."

"What Psalm would do you want me to read at the burial?" the rabbi asked him. Staring into the rabbi's thick spectacles, Jacob walked over to his mother's copy of the Torah. He opened it to a place she had marked. He remembered her reading it to him so long ago to help him fall asleep. Turning to the rabbi, he pointed to the Psalm, then let himself sink into his grandfather's chair.

The rabbi read the words:
Declare me innocent, O Lord,
For I have acted with integrity;
I have trusted in the Lord without wavering.
Put me on trial, Lord, and cross-examine me.
Test my motives and affections
For I am constantly aware of your unfailing love,
And I have lived according to your truth.

For the seven days of Shiva, the traditional period of mourning, Jacob was granted leave of duty. He spent the days sitting in his mother's garden, listening for the cooing of doves in the morning, and again, as the day ended. Each day, he cut the tear in his uniform a bit longer. By the seventh day, the coat was un-wearable.

On the eighth day, he submitted papers to his lieutenant colonel to resign his commission.

"And if I do not grant it?" the lieutenant colonel asked.

"Then I will not serve."

"Then I will have you court martialed for dereliction of duty."

"Yes, you can do that."

"A dishonorable discharge will shame your family."

"I have thought of my family's honor."

The commander's voice lowered as he realized Jacob's resolve. "Your thinking is clouded by your grief. The military is your family. How can you leave it?"

"Like this," Jacob answered. He saluted, turned sharply, and walked out the door. Outside, he paused to watch the jacaranda blossoms drop one by one.

Film Review

Five For Summer
Reviewed by Hadley Hury

Our film coverage in this Spring Issue offers our readers an opportunity to consider some recent films they may not have seen and to reconsider some older films. In hopes of piquing a variety of interests the five films have been selected to represent a range of social history and aesthetic styles. They include: a documentary focusing on the recent discovery of the work of a major 20th Century street photographer; the second, and less frequently seen, of the Astaire-Rogers films; the first English language film by a celebrated South Korean filmmaker whose work is attracting worldwide attention; a small film set in Paris and featuring two of the finest mature actors working in film today; and the mystery/legal drama—based on a famous trial for attempted murder involving Newport socialites—for which Jeremy Irons won the 1990 Academy Award for Best Actor.

LE WEEKEND (2014, Directed by Roger Michell)

The evenhanded comments of some thoughtful film critics last year regarding *Le Weekend* were popularly reduced to a meme along the lines of "dispiritingly prickly" or "a bitter pill". For those of you who may yet be wondering if perhaps whatever rankled or seemed wanting about Roger Michell's film might not be offset by Lindsay Duncan and Jim Broadbent, wonder no more: you have the right idea.

It's a small film, but its tight focus on a long-married British couple's pivotal getaway to Paris has nuanced intelligence and wit. Michell (*Hyde Park on Hudson, Notting Hill*) uses a deft, unobtrusive hand in directing Hanef Kureishi's quicksilver screenplay, and Duncan and Broadbent bring their characters to such idiosyncratic life that it's impossible to imagine anyone else in the roles.

Meg, a schoolteacher, and Nick, a philosophy professor at a provincial university, return on their thirtieth anniversary to the quaint hotel in Paris where they once enjoyed a romantic interlude. When they find that the hotel has not aged well and Meg books them into tony accommodations far beyond their means, grumpy discontents and deep veins of antagonism begin to seethe.

In the Montparnasse Cemetery Nick visits his heroes: "That was fun!" he says after paying his respects at Beckett's grave. "Let's go see Sartre!" Later, as they savor supper in a fine restaurant, he enthusiastically brings up a subject he feels is important to both of them—the new tiles for the bathroom back home. Meg wants to discuss the possibility of divorce.

The old fault lines crack open, new secrets emerge, and the world of a marriage hangs by a thread.

Whatever universal recognitions and connections may be forged will depend on the individual viewer's experience. When it tries to generalize *Le Weekend* makes a few missteps, but they are mercifully brief. The film is on its surest, most emotionally valid, footing when it trusts these two superb actors with illuminating the delicacies and ellipses of a particular marriage—not all marriages—and when it succeeds, there is hard-earned humor and a wistful, wry authenticity.

Jeff Goldblum (who is very good) enters the scene as an old college friend of Nick's—a smoothly self-aware economics pundit who now lives in Paris. He invites the couple to a celebratory soiree, and it is at the dinner table that the critical and defining moment occurs for them.

It's a subtle epiphany, the kind that might take thirty years to distill and evoke.

FINDING VIVIAN MAIER   (2013, Directed by John Maloof and Charlie Siskel)

The Work of photographer Vivian Maier is on a fast-track to critical respect and widespread popularity as a social media sensation,

but almost no one knew of it until seven years ago, and the few people who knew the artist herself were acquainted with the elusive and enigmatic woman only very minimally, very obliquely. *Finding Vivian Maier* opens with some of these people being asked to offer a one-word description of her; clearly the assignment does not come easily. After prolonged pauses of perplexed, searching consideration, each interviewee speaks: private, bold, mysterious, eccentric, paradoxical.

Maier was a willfully private person who took more than 100,000 pictures, very few of which were seen by anyone in her lifetime. Biographical research has turned-up few details of her early life. She was born in New York in 1926; lived with her mother in her native village in the French Alps in the '30s; took up work in 1951 as a nanny and soon settled in Chicago. In her free time, or even with her wards in tow, she roamed the city with a Rolleiflex camera, taking shots of people, situations, scapes, and events. The archive of her work that has come to come to light— totally by chance—is now considered by many to be among the best street photography of the 20th century.

Finding Vivian Maier is a fascinating documentary that pulls us in with a charged current of discovery; even the fact that it leaves the viewer wanting more is to its advantage—it's a tantalizing introduction to both the artist and her canon. Many of her acquaintances when she was taking some of her impactful images were the children for whom she cared. Later, when Maier was virtually destitute, some of those children took care of her, paying first for an apartment and later a nursing home, where she died at 83, in 2009, on the verge of being discovered.

For whatever reasons a loner, at once emancipated and in service, she seemed unknowable even to her upper-middle-class employers in Chicago suburbs such as Highland Park. (Class distinctions may have played a role. Her former employers presumed that so private a person would not have wanted anyone to see her photos; not one of them says that he or she ever asked Maier, with interest or encouragement, if they actually might.) Those interviewed state that she was firm but caring with their children; those children, now in late middle life, give reports of a sort of Mary Poppins with a French accent who took them on grand adventures, interspersed with one or two darker reminiscences that sharply contrast not only with the majority but with the film's generally whimsical tone and music.

The mystery began to unfold through the efforts of John Maloof who, with Charlie Siskel, co-directs the documentary. In 2007, he bought—for $380—a box of negatives at a Chicago auction; he knew only that it included street shots, a few of which he hoped might prove useful for a book he was writing. The auction house gave him Vivian Maier's name but he found not one entry for her in Google.

He later issued an appeal in Flickr; a few articles about his find appeared; and in 2011 the Chicago Cultural center mounted an exhibit, "Finding Vivian Maier: Chicago Street Photographer". Maloof, obsessed with the trove he had stumbled upon and the enigmatic artist behind it, scanned more of her work, bought more of her negatives, and went in search of anyone with whom she had crossed paths. He discovered Vivian Maier, but the Internet has made her a star.

A few of the assertions in the documentary are worrisome and a bit leering. A word of admonition, perhaps from an art historian, about our tendency to mythologize artists, particularly women artists, would have offered some helpfully balancing context. And Maloof and Siskel don't look deeply enough into what is perhaps the most incontrovertible evidence of Maier's life—the remarkable, diverse, and revealing work itself.

Nonetheless, *Finding Vivian Maier* is, from many perspectives, a must-see film; it's an engaging way to begin a journey and a shrewd consideration of the rapidly changing ways and means of assigning artistic value. It remains to be seen whether professional opinion eventually confers upon Vivian Maier's work an imprimatur that places her alongside Diane Arbus, Eugene Atget, Robert Frank, and Henri Cartier-Bresson. What has already occurred—and the excitement in watching this film—is that however those considerations pan out, we've already been admitted to the virtual museum to judge these eidetic images for ourselves.

REVERSAL OF FORTUNE (1990, Directed by Barbet Schroeder)

Director Barbet Schroeder brings a European sensibility to *Reversal of Fortune* that affords the subject the perspective it probably deserves.

His Oscar-nominated treatment urges us to take neither the bleak marital arrangements of Claus and Sunny von Bulow nor the legalistic grandstanding of attorney Alan Dershowitz too seriously. His focus is on gamesmanship. The rules—of both society and personal conduct—are examined dispassionately. And it's a level playing field: no cheap shots at the rich are allowed, and there is only a cool respect, not righteous reverence, for the law.

Schroeder and screenwriter Nicholas Kazan, working from actual transcripts of the notorious trial and Dershowitz's own account of the proceedings (his book of the same title was published in 1986), clearly know that what they have on their hands is a superb mystery. Eschewing both tabloid luridness and moral presumption, they fashion the mixed motives, circumstantial evidence, and inherent grotesqueries of the case into a mordantly humorous entertainment.

Irons.jpg As Claus von Bulow, the mysterious opportunist married to Newport heiress Sunny and convicted of twice trying to kill her by insulin injection, Jeremy Irons is the film's richest treat. His von Bulow is robustly chill. This was Irons' most complex performance to date (he won the Best Actor Oscar and Golden Globe)—a reach that was large both physically and vocally, yet managed with intricate subtlety. Perhaps his most impressive feat is modulating his characteristically sensitive intelligence into something radically

different—something shrewd and inscrutable, more blockish and literal. The voice is also transformed: it's deeper, rounder, and has the stolid cadence of a world-weary but socially correct Teutonic sensualist.

Irons is particularly funny when his von Bulow tries for a sort of hail-fellow, Gary Cooperish delivery in his talks with Dershowitz (Ron Silver). We begin to look forward to his would-be expansiveness and his occasional jokes that are surprisingly touching in their wry innocence. It is Irons who largely drives the movie, providing its essential mystery, humor, and unpredictability. He nails the overweening *self-possession* of von Bulow—the central enigma that is fundamental to the story.

Somewhat similarly, Glenn Close dulls her usual spark in rendering Sunny von Bulow as an alcoholic money-puppet. It's an unsympathetic portrait of a woman whose marked indifference to life, her children, and the opportunities of wealth and privilege is numbing in its vacuous self-destructiveness. Close does manage to eke some colorings of human feelings for her character in a couple of scenes where we sense that she may indeed have been victimized (beyond her own missteps) by her fortune. She creates an absorbing portrayal of the society beauty, now aging, retreating from her millions and her misalliances—in a frumpy Wasp cardigan and a drunken stumble—to her last resort, a closely guarded bathroom stocked with pills.

Ron Silver as Alan Dershowitz, the celebrity Harvard law professor who represented Klaus, has a feverish energy that provides the counterbalance for hanging the tale. His scenes with the stable of star law students he hastily assembles to prepare for the second trial have the slick, suspenseful pace of a good documentary. Silver's may be a larger role than that of Irons or Close, but his manic lawyering feels more like a foil for their showier turns. He is always a reliably realistic actor, and director Schroeder enriches the interplay here by dramatically juxtaposing Silver's naturalistic common man against Irons' and Close's beautifully stylized rendition of the von Bulows.

Schroeder and Kazan successfully blend some fictional assumptions with multifaceted source materials. The cast, all at the top of their game, deliver performances sharpened by intuition and technical virtuosity. The cinematography of Luciano Totvolo has an old-money sheen and Mark Isham's score a glacial elegance. The film's sophisticated *sang-froid* creeps up on you like a hard frost in the night.

SNOWPIERCER (2014, Directed by Joon-ho Bong)

Snowpiercer was positioned in last summer's market as more intellectual and stylish than competing futuristic and/or blunt-force action thrillers. This comparison is not completely earned, despite the sometimes interesting work of hot director Joon-ho Bong who also did the screenplay adaptation from a 1982 graphic novel, *Le Transperceneige*. The source material plays right into Bong's vaunted dedication to careful composition and capacious framing. Though the film is perversely overlong and its palette wearyingly dark, there is a meticulousness (if not always clarity) in the narrative that outstrips the chaotic overload of many films taken from comic books.

A dystopian moral parable, *Snowpiercer* picks up 17 years after a

misbegotten attempt to reverse the final throes of global warming—a chemical was released into the atmosphere and overcorrects: a second ice age has ensued and wiped out all life on the planet. As luck would have it, an eccentric trillionaire named Wilford (Ed Harris) had already completed work on a long and uncannily efficient self-sustaining train. He allows the world's few hundred survivors to board his ark-like vehicle—which travels the world on an endless loop—so long as they stay in their "preordained places".

A cruel apartheid is sustained by the authoritarian regime: the decadent one-percenters live in luxury in the front cars, and the poor and dispossessed are crammed into the rear. Thereby hangs the Darwinian/Orwellian allegory about political inequality and wealth disparity; until Curtis, played by Chris Evans ("Captain America", "The Avengers") decides it's time to lead a revolt. His comrades in strategy and arms include the ever estimable John Hurt, Octavia Spencer, and "Billy Elliot's" Jamie Bell, an interesting and versatile actor who's overdue for more challenging roles.

The film's only vitality and wit emanate from Tilda Swinton's sly performance as Mason, a bureaucratic functionary who shuttles between the mysterious and unseen Wilford, in the inner sanctum of the "sacred engine" at the front of the train, and her periodic speeches to the hoi polloi. Her admonitions to the underlings are the only unadulterated jewels of black comedy admitted to the film's prevailing gloom. The surety of tone and rhetoric—quite obviously patterned on Margaret Thatcher's—has a fey hilarity. Her condescension is wedded to her belief in the absolute necessity of everyone being kept in his appropriate and "divinely designated" place; it is a seamless ideology, unwittingly despicable and robustly forthright. In one of these ghoulish homilies she reminds the huddled masses, using one of the unfortunates as a model for the lesson, that, "We are the head. You are the foot. You would not put a shoe on your head, would you? Would you!"

Only near the end of the film do we see any scenes of the life in the forward cars—and it seems a missed opportunity for opening things up, not only for the thematic contrast but for a bit more visual and emotional breath. *Snowpiercer* is aggressively bleak, the only action that occurs is violent, and the film's unrelieved dimness begins to work against its apparent aim: rather than steadily accruing sympathy for the horribly treated underclasses, viewers are more likely to become impatient and inured.

Bong's penchant for storyboarding every frame of his films is nowhere more evident than in the scenes of violent brutality. Along with an assortment of tortures and mistreatments along the way, there are three excruciatingly protracted set-pieces of battle as, car by car, the rebelling back-of-the-trainers make their way forward and engage with their oppressors. The camera leers lustfully as—often in close-up—a highly orchestrated maelstrom of bodies is variously axed, speared, gouged, and otherwise sliced and diced.

That these overlong (sometimes slow-motion) scenes are among the most reverentially staged is indicative of what's most wrongheaded and disagreeable about Bong's film. He has some flair for treating timely and provocative themes with serious thought and a rich cinematic sense comprising pictorial vividness with narrative verve and velocity; unfortunately, here both the central metaphor and the filmic scope and storytelling are beaten to a very slow death. We might look forward to Bong taking a good idea, drilling deeper and with more economy, and focusing his talents to more compelling effect. The problem with *Snowpiercer* is that its apocalyptic take on humanity at its basest is too long, too underdeveloped, and too unrelentingly grim. The film suffers from the very vision it depicts—life bereft of all but its most depraved instinct for survival, with no remaining vestige of animating spirit, and even sensation jaded beyond numbness.

THE GAY DIVORCEE (1934, Directed by Mark Sandrich)

Fred Astaire and Ginger Rogers were initially teamed in *Flying Down to Rio* in 1933, but this feature was their first effort together as stars—and it's tremendous fun. Based on Dwight Taylor and Cole Porter's play of the same name, *The Gay Divorcee* centers on Mimi (Rogers), a woman seeking a divorce from her husband. She travels to an English seaside resort, pursued by the love-stricken Guy (Astaire), whom she mistakes for the hired correspondent in her divorce case. Among the many musical numbers are Porter's gorgeous "Night and Day," the only song from the original Broadway musical included in the film, and Con Conrad and Herb Magidson's "The Continental," which won the first ever Academy Award for Best Song.

Like most of the Fred and Ginger films the plot of *The Gay Divorcee* is as evanescent as champagne froth; as usual the mistaken identities and motives, cross-purposes, and romantic banter whimsically concoct the merest pretext for the real feast—the dancing, Van Nest Polglase's late art deco scenic design, and the delectable performances of the supporting cast. The work of the character actors here is so expert and so rich it's as essential to the film's charm as that of the leads. Indeed, when characters have names such as Hortense Ditherwell—Mimi's aunt, played by Alice Brady— and Egbert "Pinky" Fitzgerald (the distinctively hilarious Edward Everett Horton, who appeared in two other Fred and Ginger movies), we might think we've wandered into a Restoration comedy—and we

wouldn't be far wrong. There's even an Italian singing lothario named Rodolfo Tonetti (Erik Rhodes, who has an archetypal perfection). The laughs in *The Gay Divorcee* derive at times from arch silliness, at others from innuendo so sly as to seem almost subliminal.

In his long career Horton almost always played in droll counterpoint to the male lead, most often as a supercilious personal secretary or valet or, as here, an effete gentleman. (His particular talent and the persona of his roles of the '30s and '40s prefigure some of the superb Tony Randall's performances with Doris Day and Rock Hudson/James Garner in the late '50s and '60s.) Horton has scenes in *The Gay Divorcee* which actors still study as mini-classes in the difficult art of comedy: his timing and subtlety are breathtaking and he was a master of the necessity in comedy for absolutely serious sincerity. His scene with a head waiter played by the brilliant Eric Blore—who also appears in three other Fred and Ginger vehicles—is a joy forever for film buffs and one from which many can quote at length. (see—http://www.youtube.com/watch?v=Y9fHz8fOIPQ)

The Gay Divorcee was nominated for the Best Picture Oscar in 1935. Other highlights include another swell Magidson-Conrad tune for Astaire, "Needle in a Haystack", and a poolside Horton—togged-out in Edwardian bathing costume—with a featured 17-year-old Betty Grable in a camp dance number, "Let's K-Knock K-Knees".

What's not to like?

Poetry

Three Poems by Daniel Barbare

Whitman's Sampler

2 pounds 8 ozs. Box. Bluebird.
Basket of flowers. Coconut.
Caramel. Molasses Chew.
Maple Fudge. Toffee. Pecans
and English Walnut Cluster.
Vanilla Butter Cream. Fruit and
Nut Caramel. Cashew Cluster.
Chocolate Truffle. Chocolate
Whip. Milk Chocolate
Messenger Boy. Chocolate
Covered Almonds. Chocolate
Covered Peanuts. And not but
least Cherry Cordials.

To the Rescue

Hilton brand. 5.99 a container. Southern
Homes cocktail sauce.
Slippery oyster on a fork and
dipped and down the throat. The
fishy ocean on my breath. As
Coca-Cola to the rescue
and two pieces of Whitman's chocolates.

The Mouse in the House

The tiny blur all fuzzy
and gray. Around the kitchen
counter. Stops. Looks with
big eyes. Runs behind the
couch. Around the Christmas
tree all aglow in the den. Goes
behind the TV. Towards the
hearth. Makes a quick u-turn
on those silent little feet. My
wife as if to tiptoe and scream
and shout in the house.

Short Story

Beatle Boots
By Les Bohem

I met Heather Allen on my second day of summer camp. Two days earlier, my parents had taken me to the Burbank Airport and deposited me on the plane for Reno with about twelve other kids. In Reno, we were met by Ray, a counselor who wore two-hundred-dollar cowboy boots and chewed tobacco. He drove us in his pickup to the Walking G Ranch, a mile outside Taylorsville, California. The Walking G bred jumping horses and every summer part of their grounds was turned into a camp. It was a large spread against the side of the Taylorsville River.

The woods and mountains of northern California surrounded the ranch. Mount Lassen National Park was less than sixty miles away. I was thirteen and had just finished my first year of junior high school; I wasn't at all interested in the bounty of God's creation.

What I was interested in, so much so that everything else in the world might as well have been the background blur of an out-of-focus snapshot, was the Beatles. They had appeared to me like a vision during my first awful days of junior high. There was nothing as bad as junior high school, and the first days were the bottom of that incredibly deep barrel. Today, if I were given a choice between living as a heretic during the Spanish Inquisition or reliving the first two weeks of junior high, I would rush for the rack with arms outstretched. I often think that the kindest thing we could do for our children is to take them out and promptly shoot them on their graduation from the sixth grade.

The tortures were many. There were the bullies, older kids who threw pennies at you and wrote huge S's on your back in chalk to mark you as a seventh-grade "scrub." There were sweet talkers who sold you tickets to the third-floor swimming pool when there was no third floor. There were the unhelpful teachers, all of whom hated junior high school more than you ever would, and the ungodly routine of moving from class to class. There were the fights and the crushes and the panic when you lost some card or other that your father was supposed to sign. More than anything else, there was the newness, and a vague anxiety to go with it. Junior high school began the business of growing up, and it must have been that, more than anything else, that was what made the whole thing so frightening.

I had gone through my first week in the abyss and saw no hope of ever climbing out, when I heard "Love Me Do" on the radio. There was something in that record, as there was in all the ones that would follow, that was a salve against the wounds of day-to-day life. I think it was the promise of never-never land. The Beatles were Peter Pan come to give all of us Wendys one last chance to fly. We didn't have to get serious, to think about our future, to grow up. We could stay outside and play for a little while longer.

By the end of the year, the Beatles had become a fixture in my life, an immovable point around which everything else turned. I had all their records, I knew the words to every song, I wanted to grow up to be John Lennon. The beauties of mountain and stream held little attraction for me. The only enticement that my parents could offer me for going to camp was that my friend, Andy, would also be there.

Andy and I had gone to grammar school together and our parents were friends. We'd been separated by our districts and were going to different junior highs, but we had seen a lot of each other during the year. Andy had a drum set on which he could keep a pretty good beat, and he could toss his hair just like Ringo. We were still very good friends.

But Andy had gone with his parents to New York, and he would be coming to camp a week late. For that first week, I was to be on my own.

At thirteen, I was the oldest of the campers by a year. It was a year that made a lot of difference. After the trials of junior high school, the sixth graders seemed loud and silly. Already on the truck ride from the airport, I had decided that I wasn't going to make any new friends.

We got to camp around dinnertime. Several other truckloads of campers had already arrived. It was dark by the time we finished eating. Ray led the way back from the mess hall to the boys' cabin.

It was a long room of about fifteen bunk beds, with a bathroom and a shower at one end. I took the top bunk at the far end of the room and put my duffel bag on the bunk below, to save it for Andy.

Ray slept in the cabin with us, in a separate area that was partitioned off. The partition only went up about two-thirds of the way to the ceiling, and Ray's reading lamp would light the room in a faint glow after lights-out. Ray also had a record player in his "room." And a guitar. That first night, he sang us to sleep with Hank Williams songs, and in the morning, we woke up to a record of George Jones singing, "The Race Is On."

There was no schedule for the first full day of camp. We were supposed to walk around, get familiar with our surroundings and with each other.

I ate breakfast quickly and then started out by myself. I went into the woods beyond the mess hall and came to the river. I followed the river upstream for a while and then wandered away toward a barn.

The barn door was open and I went inside. It was a hot day, but the barn was cool. A huge mound of hay filled the place, and a rope hung from the rafters. I lay down in the hay and two things happened. I sneezed and someone laughed. I sat up quickly and looked around me. I couldn't see anyone.

"Hey, toss me that rope."

It was a girl's voice coming from somewhere above me. I stood up and looked around. Heather Allen was sitting on a crossbeam, almost straight over my head. She was in jeans, a bright red T-shirt, and her hair was the same dirty yellow as the hay. I grabbed the end of the rope and tossed it up. It took me three tries to get it to her, then she caught it and in the same motion came back down with it, landing next to me in the hay. I sneezed again.

"'ts your name?" she asked me, pulling some hay out of her hair.

We stayed in the barn for about an hour. Heather was fourteen and her father was the Walking G wrangler. She lived there all year and she hated the summers because of the campers.

"Someday I'm going to make a lot of money and buy this place and none of you sons of bitches'll get past the damn gate," she said.

We took turns on the rope, dropping into the hay. My eyes were running and I was sneezing. She teased me about it and said it showed how much I knew. I trembled a little climbing out on the beam to catch the rope and I hoped she didn't notice. She had a rich, wild laugh and the most wonderful eyes in the world. They were blue and they danced and shimmered.

After a while we both lay back in the hay, tired. Neither of us said anything. We were there for about ten minutes when a man's voice called from outside.

"Heather? Heather?"

"Hey," she whispered to me. "You're not supposed to be over here. You're all right though. What bunk've you got?"

"The last one back on the right, by the window."

"Top or bottom?"

"Top."

"All right, I'll come get you tonight."

She looked at me for a minute. My eyes were watering again. She took my hand and put my finger under my nose.

"For Christ's sake don't sneeze."

She smiled and left.

I waited for about twenty minutes and then walked back to camp. I felt a lot of things at once. Nervous, because I would have to sneak out of the cabin that night, and because I was afraid she might not come. Important, because Heather was the prettiest girl I'd ever seen and she seemed to like me. Self-conscious, because hay made me sneeze and I was a year younger, and climbing out on beams and sneaking out of the cabin were things that made me nervous and I wanted, more than anything in the world, to be whatever it was that Heather Allen wanted.

After dinner, we had a bonfire and one of the counselors told stories. It was a warm evening with a breeze, the sky staying deep blue. I didn't listen to the stories.

When it was time to go to bed, we walked back to the cabin with Ray leading us. I was in my bunk before most of the other kids were out of the shower. The bonfire had lasted a long time and I was afraid that I'd missed Heather. I lay there and waited. Soon all the others were back in their bunks. Ray took a head count and then went behind his partition. He began to softly play the guitar and sing. The others drifted to sleep. I picked up my jeans and put them back on. I held my shirt under my sleeping bag.

I lay there for a long time. I hoped that Ray would finish before Heather came, but he seemed to know every song ever written. I had begun to think that she wasn't coming when I felt a breeze from the opened window behind me. I hadn't heard a thing.

"C'mon," Heather whispered.

Quietly, I slipped out of my sleeping bag and started out the window. Ray was still singing behind me. My jeans caught on a nail and my foot kicked against the wall. It was a loud noise. Someone coughed. Ray stopped singing. I froze with my head out the window. I could see Heather below me, waiting.

51

"Hurry up," she said.

I made a face and reached back, trying to find the nail and unhook my jeans. Ray started a new song and I freed myself. I jumped out the window and stood on the ground facing Heather.

I pulled on my shirt and she took my hand and led me across the field toward the river. We went into the woods. There had been a moon but it was already down under the trees and the night was dark. She knew her way and walked quickly, dragging me behind her.

"Scared?" she asked.

I said that I wasn't. I was thinking about her hand. I squeezed a little. She squeezed mine back.

We got to the river and she led me along the bank, until we got to a big slab of rock set like a shelf above the water. We sat down. The rock was cool, and without our footsteps, the night was full of its own sounds. Heather leaned into the water and pulled out two bottles of beer. She reached into her jeans pocket and took out a bottle opener.

"I get these from the guys in town," she said. "Ricky steals them from the market."

She handed me an opened bottle and sat close to me, so that my arm was practically around her. I had never had a beer before. We drank for a little while in silence, and then she turned and looked at me. Her face was very close to mine. I put down my beer and kissed her.

Her mouth was cool from the beer. I remember that most of all. The wet coolness that matched the cool of the rock and the summer night.

Heather was the first girl I had ever kissed and I was worried that she would say something, tease me the way she had about sneezing. She must have known, but she didn't say anything. We kissed for a while and then drank some more beer and then kissed again. Then we sat back and looked at the stars. There were a lot of things that I knew would one day happen to me without really believing that that day would ever come. I would grow up, go to college, have to shave every day, get married, have children, die. I realized that one of those things had happened.

After a while, she got up and led the way back to the cabin. It was much harder to climb in the window than it had been to climb out. She had to put her hands together and boost me up. Ray's light was out and the room was dark. There was the quiet sound of a lot of people sleeping. When I leaned out the window to look for Heather, she had gone.

The next day we went riding. I had never been on a horse and I was put in the beginners' group. I spent the day hoping that Heather wouldn't see me struggling with my horse. After dinner, I went straight back to the cabin and waited. She didn't come.

The day after that we drove up into the hills and swam in a lake. We got back in the early afternoon. I walked up to the barn and started in. One of the wranglers yelled at me and sent me back to camp. Heather didn't come that night either.

The next night, I was almost asleep when I felt the breeze behind me. Ray was singing behind his partition. I pulled on my jeans and climbed out the window.

We went back to the rock by the river. I wanted to ask her where she'd been for the last two days, but I didn't. I told her stories about my friend Andy and I told her about the Beatles.

"I've never heard them," she said. "But Ricky says they're queer."

"No, they're not. John Lennon's married."

"I don't care. The guys in town like Roy Orbison. They're not going to play no Beatles at the Fourth of July dance."

Below the rock, the water was deep enough to swim in. We swam in our underwear. There was something unfamiliar in the cool, dark water. We swam and we talked and we kissed, and it was nearly dawn when I got back to the cabin.

The next day was Friday. I didn't see Heather. On Saturday we walked into town with Ray. He was picking up supplies. One of the other counselors met us there with the truck.

Taylorsville was a tiny town with a main street where there was a market, a gas station, and an American Legion auditorium. Outside the auditorium was a huge banner advertising the Fourth of July dance.

Ray bought us each a soft drink. I was hot from the walk and I sat on the porch by the market to drink mine.

Across the street by the auditorium were three huge Indians smoking cigarettes. They were boys, about sixteen, and as big as anyone I'd ever seen. They wore jeans and Levi's jackets with the sleeves cut off. A fourth, dressed just like his friends, came out of the market and crossed the street. He had two watermelons under each arm.

He caught me staring at him and he looked at me for a moment and then he laughed. It was the meanest sound I had ever heard.

Heather came for me again on Sunday night. She seemed different. She was very serious.

She took my hand right away and we started walking for the rock.

"Don't say anything," she said, and squeezed my hand.

We walked through the woods to the rock and sat down. Heather looked at me and put her hand in the water.

"Do a lot of kids go to your school?" she asked.

"I guess."

"I don't think I'd like it in L.A. You can't have a horse there."

"People have horses."

She was quiet. She looked away from me, then cupped her hands and splashed water into her face. She never looked prettier to me than she did then.

***

Andy came late Monday night. One of the counselors had driven to Reno to get him. He was wearing Beatle boots. They were the most wonderful things I had ever seen. Black and shiny with pointed toes and elastic on the sides. His mother had bought them for him in New York, from the shop that made them for the Beatles.

We made plans that night. I was going to get an electric guitar as soon as I could. Andy already had the drums. We would form a band.

The next morning at breakfast, Ray sat down with the two of us.

"Since you two are the oldest here," he said, "we kind of figured you might like to go to the Fourth of July dance in town. It should be a lot of fun."

Andy had brought The Beatles' Second Album. I hadn't heard it yet. Ray said that we could listen to it on his record player. I ran up to the barn. The wrangler who had thrown me out was there. I told him that I was looking for Heather. He said that she was at the stable. I found her and brought her back to the cabin.

We sat in Ray's room and listened to the record. Andy would turn up his favorite parts. Heather didn't seem to like him much. When I asked him to, he showed her his Beatle boots, which he had put under his bunk so they wouldn't get dirty. She said that she liked cowboy boots better.

When the first side of the record was over, she stood up.

"It's not very good," she said and walked out.

I followed her outside. I caught up with her and tried to hold her hand. She pulled away.

"What's the matter?"

"Nothing."

"Hey, me and Andy are going to the Fourth of July dance. I thought we could all go together."

"I don't know if I'm going."

She ran back toward the stables. I went inside and listened to the other side of the album with Andy. It sounded tinny and far away through Ray's little speaker.

Andy was very excited about the dance. He thought that he might meet a girl there. In New York he had stayed with his mother's sister's family. His aunt had a daughter his own age, and the daughter had a girlfriend.

"I think we're sort of going steady," he said. "I'm doing pretty good so far this summer."

I tried to find Heather the next day, but she wasn't at the stables. She didn't come that night.

The day after that was the Fourth. Andy spent the morning polishing his boots, which were already shiny and clean. We went riding that afternoon. When we came back to the cabin, Andy's boots were gone.

Andy started to cry, and the other kids gathered around. Ray came out and I told him what happened. He spoke sternly to all of us about taking someone else's property. Then he went through everyone's bunk and duffel bag. There were no boots.

Andy didn't go to dinner. He didn't want to go to the dance either, but Ray said that he had to.

We drove into town with Ray and two of the girls' counselors. We parked by the market and walked across the street to the dance. The auditorium was lit up brightly, and there were no other lights on in the town.

There were about forty people in the hall. It was decorated in red, white, and blue crepe paper. A jukebox played country music and old rock and roll. I looked around the room for Heather. She wasn't there. Outside, someone was shooting off firecrackers.

Ray was dancing with one of the counselors. Andy hadn't said a word. He walked over and sat by the punch bowl. The other counselor asked me to dance.

She was very nice. She was twenty and waiting to dance with Ray. We went onto the dance floor. I was still looking for Heather. Outside, the firecrackers were getting louder. About halfway through the song, I saw something shiny and familiar at my feet. It was Andy's Beatle boot. I looked up. Dancing next me, wearing the boots, was an Indian boy, about my age. He had on a sleeveless Levi's jacket.

He had seen me looking at the boots. When the song ended, he started for the door. I went after him without saying a word to the counselor.

He was outside the door when I got there, just to one side.

"Where'd you get those boots?"

"Eat it."

"Those are my friend's boots."

Another voice came from somewhere behind me.

"Those are my brother's boots."

I turned around and the Indian I'd seen carrying the watermelons was standing behind me. His three friends came from behind the auditorium. Heather was with them.

"You want them back?" he asked me.

Heather looked right at me and smiled a tough smile. I was frightened. I could feel myself starting to cry. I didn't want them to see that. I turned and walked quickly back into the building.

Andy was still sitting by the punch bowl. He looked up as I came in.

"I bet it was that girl that took them," he said. I felt too guilty to look at him.

The counselor asked me to dance again, and then she danced with Ray and I danced with the other counselor. Andy stayed in his seat by the punch bowl. Outside, the firecrackers had stopped.

***

I only saw Heather once after that. It was about a week later. We were out riding and we'd stopped in a field to have lunch. There was the sound of a galloping horse and Heather rode past us. The sun was bright and her yellow hair caught the light. She disappeared quickly up a hill.

A few nights later I woke up, feeling a breeze behind me. When I reached for the window, it was closed. I still kept my jeans at the foot of the bunk. I slipped them on and climbed out the window.

It was a bright night, with a nearly full moon. I walked through the woods toward the river. There was nobody on the rock. I sat for a while, listening to the river and the crickets. Finally I got up and took my pocketknife out. I walked back into the woods and, picking a tree that could not easily be seen from the river, I carved Heather's name and my own into its side. My knife was small and its blade was dull and it took me nearly until morning to finish carving.

Poetry

Inattentive You by Tobi Cogswell

Inattentive You

You're the kind of father
who rides up the hill in front,
and never looks back.
You don't even know if your son
is wearing his helmet,
or if he is off his bike
running to catch up with you.

You're the kind of father
who loudly watches
the most violent movies.
You don't even know that your son
is peeking from around the corner,
or that he tosses uneasily at night,
hoping the terror changes to peace.
You won't even know when your son
hits someone at school.

You're the kind of father
who will stay out until dark.
You don't even know that your son
stands by the window, missing you so badly,
wondering what he's done wrong.

You're the kind of father
who invites judgment
by someone much more important
than I.

Poetry

Five Poems by Mark Mansfield

Uncle Siddhartha

The future's just coming for a visit,
dragging along that cat of a different stripe.
Meanwhile outside of the once-thriving mining camp
of Grand Nuance,
you've been nabbed
comparing more apples and oranges.

Scattered reports have also resurfaced
of your being spied chasing rainbows
out behind the Old McDonald place,
while on at least one occasion you were spotted
catching a falling star
without putting it in your pocket.

Needless to say,
we have had it with you.
This time we intend on taping your mouth shut for good
with soap.

Oh yes, you will be worse
than sorry.   God may even lead another
one of his Victory Parades,
                                            cartwheels turning
somersaults and everyone crossing that bridge

over Spilt Milk Canyon.

The Straw Room Mambo

Rude awakenings happen upon you
with more frequency than zombie extras
doing zombie-ons
in *The Night of the Living Dead.*

A cross-eyed pessimist, your upper lip's
usually about as stiff as a Shirley Temple
with the extra cherry.

Old Mother Hubbard's your patron saint
and her dog, Cupboard's
your guardian angel.

Wandering gamely as a cloud,
you recently awoke to find yourself
strapped to a gurney while your *Doppelgänger*
and the ER staff finished wolfing down cake emblazoned:

> *Happy Birthday, Markles!!!*

For you, the glass has never been so much
half-empty or half-full
                              as typically aimed at your skull
by one of life's less amiable patrons.

Next to you,
Rumpelstiltskin was Mister Rogers.

Skunked

Love doesn't mean never having to say
you're sorry; love means being sorrier than
you would ever have thought imaginable.
Got a few likes and dislikes?   Forget that.
Love means to have you nodding like a windsock
every other waking moment whilst you assent
to harebrained schemes, half-baked notions, pie-in-
the-sky pipe dreams, I'll-have-my-cake-and-get-
yours, too, rhetorical cookoffs, plus the odd
bout of full-throttled lunacy. Love conjures
any and all of the following pleasantries:
socializing with those you'd just as lief
nudge in the path of a basilisk; summarily
relocating somewhere in the environs of
ultima Thule; and/or divesting yourself
of any shreds remaining from your formerly
so-so life prior to morphing into
a human Smiley Face. Typically, love
loves showing its own smarmy puss
whenever, wherever, and however it damned
well feels like: curdled pop ditties, winsome
soaps operas, bodice rippers, artsy-fartsy
masterworks, poetry, and the like,
all fairly ooze with the stuff, largely due
to our peculiarly persistent mania
for divorcing ourselves from reality
almost as often as from each other. Love, O, over-
reaching, overbearing, overpublicized
Love! careless as you are—why's it so few
ever truly give you the old heave-ho?

Useful Insights

>   *Someone*
> *is thinking of you without*
> *being aware of it.*
>   Amy Gerstler

Let's try another example.
It's Wednesday,
late evening,
the planets and stars,
the moon most probably
are out there trining, sextiling,
etc., so that you can enjoy a meal with friends,
but don't overeat or spend too much.

You are sensitive to your surroundings now
and may have useful insights.
Why not make a to-do list of household chores?

Might you feel better
if you let someone get close?

The Lost Cause Saloon

Deciding to make camp here for the night,
you plop your ass down in the least-lit booth
right by the shitter in the old Lost Cause Saloon.
First tossing back a few perfunctory shots
of Rebel Yell faster than Grant took Richmond,
you attempt to saunter toward the Rock-Ola
as if your name were Lyle or Vern, and you
damned well fucking meant to spill your drink,
as well as every bit of change you own,
along with your keys, credit cards, two M
&Ms, and a napkin from another bar
whereon is scrawled apparently what could be
part of someone's phone number, or name.
Casually picking your crap up off the floor,
you start to scrutinize the juke, while trying
to figure out precisely why ZZ Top
and Skynyrd never merged, so every frigging
selection then could be by "Skynyrd Top"
or "ZZ Skyn," perhaps. Still swilling down
the contents of your empty glass, you opt
for Don and Phil, soon joining the two of them
in elegiacally bleating out "Dreeeaammmm,
                              dream, dream, dream, dream,"
while poking at the word REPLAY until it breaks.

By now, feeling pretty maudlin in a shit-
faced sort of way, you note the rebel sentries,
posted, keg-like bellies to the bar,
and disguised as denim- and leather-clad bikers,
all tarted up, sporting colors which read,
Confederate Nose Punchers, Cooterville
and who have begun to slowly start to move
their hirsute lips en masse while staring holes
through you the size of Scooter Pies and looking
increasingly like the mullet Mafia.

Determined to try to elude Goober Patrol,
you manage to stumble outdoors on to what

appears to be The Smallest Parking Lot
in the Northern Hemisphere, where you spy
one of the sentries' mounts still idling.
Hi Ho Silvering your ass astraddle "Traveler,"
you wheelie halfway round the lot before
you surface near enough semi-consciousness
to conclude you never really did much care
for *The Wild One*—or *Easy Rider*
for that matter, as you start to clutch while choking
the bejesus out of your handlebar-like reins
(and broncing your sorry ass very near
perpendicular) while more and more
roundless doughnuts pockmark the lot, with you
now fanning more clouds of gravel, sand, and dirt
than a drunken posse at high noon, seconds
before one of the gnarlier-looking sentries
wildly charges out of The Lost Cause, grabs
a-hold of your magic reins, then rains the first
of many well-aimed nose punches down on Yankee
Doodle You.

Short Story

The Red Light
By Ivan Alexander

He could hear distant sirens, and wondered if he should pull over. The yellow traffic light ahead was turning red, so he stopped at the intersection instead. At the light he waited, the sirens grew louder. Bear earned his nickname back at the 753rd Ordnance Disposal, EOD in West Virginia, and it had stuck ever since. He was a congenial fellow and well liked. His frame loomed large on the field, hunched over a project, which is why his team mates had given him his endearing name, Bear. Now with many missions of bomb disposal behind him, it had become as much a part of him as his large steady hands, strong fingers, and he thought about that now. Bear was about to neutralize a newly discovered improvised explosive ordnance near the entrance venue at Yankee Stadium. It was deemed too sensitive to move, so his EOD was called. That evening's game with the Dodgers was postponed until Ordnance gave the 'all clear' signal. It appeared a homemade bomb, but unfamiliar.

Bear had seen many devices, some more clever than others, some he would rather forget. All were diffused. But this IED was a new design. The trigger mechanism behind the outer casing cover was electrical; he knew that. It puzzled him why the inner casing had a flashing red light, which usually meant a timer. None was evident here. It resembled a simple 555 relay with both red and green LED lights, but different somehow. On one hand it appeared obviously simple; on the other it was remarkably well hidden, a sinister Chinese box hiding its true intent. He paused and watched, taking in his breath slowly to steady himself. Who, what fiendish mind, would install such a devious trigger, so simple yet so complex, he wondered silently. Everyone else at risk, including his team, were safely back of the hastily erected barricades, so he was all alone in his work. It was a job, his duty, and he was proud to do it. Saving lives was part of his training; it was also in his character.

Time was fading into dark, and Bear knew many children were eager for the game, adult fans too. It briefly reminded him when he played little league back home in the foothills of Virginia, the small diamond field framed by the large blue mountains beyond. It gave him a momentary reassurance, but his training taught him to bracket the thought and move it safely aside. His thoughts had to focus directly on the dangerous task at hand without distraction. There were audible murmurs behind him, just beyond the barricades, police chatter. He knew how high was the tension there, having been an observer himself on other missions, tense, crouching, listening. He was crouching now, his large bulk armored in helmet and torso protecting armor, gloves removed as he worked his tools. A bolt was unwound a quarter turn, listening for a click. No sounds. He turned it again a quarter. By now beads of perspiration had formed around his eyes, and they stung a little. But Bear paid it no mind. It was impossible to reach inside the helmet's thick visor. In response he again steadied himself, unconsciously counting each breath as if it were his last. He was extra careful with the wire crossing over another, as their ends were exposed. He felt a vice tighten around his heart. A spark would be fatal. He finally removed the inner casing over the trigger, very carefully and deliberately he set it aside on the tarp. Then his fingers gently probed deeper into the mechanism, red light still flashing.

There was a large red wire showing, obviously a decoy, and two lesser ones in yellow and blue, begging innocence, but he was not tempted to use his cutter on any of them. Rather, he pushed them aside for a better view, back behind the small nine volt battery. Hidden there was the key to dismantling this trigger, he thought. You have to think like a bomb maker, imagine his devious mind working in solitude, the monster chortling to himself. How many people will his evil creation kill? How much terror will it spread? He had to imagine it studiously like that. But instead he imagined his father and himself setting traps by the creek, remembering the beavers they caught. The branch down from their house would flood at times, and it was always the beavers. He remembered his father, tall and strong... But again he dismissed the thought and counted his breath. There was no time to reflect now, all that is passed. A few inches from his face was the deadly bomb that needed dismantling, and he needed more light.

There was the pressure of time, the mysterious red light, the crossed wires, the beads of sweat, his rapid breathing, growing darkness; all weighed on Bear as he probed deeper with his instruments, trying to get a clearer view. Minutes seemed like hours. He set them aside to light another torch, moving it into place for its strong beam to better focus on the IED's trigger. Behind the barricades were flashing red and blue lights of emergency vehicles, casting fleeting shadows around him, dark silhouettes of his large hunched figure. He could hear a chopper high overhead. Bear finally understood the deviously treacherous mind of its maker, how he wired the trigger with a clever devil's bargain: Either wire, blue or yellow, could trigger the mechanism; or it could stop the bomb. Bear let out a long held breath, almost a whistle through his teeth, his steady hand betraying a slight tremor. Which wire to cut? Everything now hinged on this choice. He tensed: Which one?

Bear had been here before, back in training at Quantico. He remembered vaguely the same choice presented during exercise. He chose rightly then; time fading like a dying ember, he must do it again. As his concentration deepened, the ambient background noise faded into silent calm. Incongruously, he saw his wife Mary and their little girl Sam, her golden hair playing in the sunlight. Was it an apparition? He could not dismiss them, but cautiously moved the thought aside.

 He felt his fingers close on the wire cutter, squeezing, softly squeezing the blades to cut. Bear stopped, listening to his breath, making certain it was the right thing. He squeezed further... To his surprise, the LED turned green.

The traffic light was green. He felt his foot on the accelerator... He never heard the loud bang.

Poetry

Two Poems by J.H. Johns

Jury Duty

I got the letter
in the mail—
for jury duty;

but, it seems,
they don't understand
that I'm maxed out
on being in the jury box;

watching the government kill
my friends and buddies
in Viet Nam;

watching my own number
come up;

watching a bunch of bankrupt people
try and cripple an entire generation;

watching my father die
from a form of leukemia
because he shoveled uranium
for the Department of Energy;

no,
they *really* don't understand;

I've seen enough—

I've had my fill of
"jury duty"
to last a lifetime—

no thanks…

yeah,
I've done my jury duty;
I've sat there,
and after due deliberations,
I found all those people in my life
"not guilty"
and undeserving
of the death penalty…

Safety Deposit

They kept the peace,
to get their piece
of contents unknown;

cramped in a small room,
both womb and tomb;
waiting for the unknown;

they opened the locks,
they took out the box,
eyes wide for the unknown;

slowly lifting the lid,
both rabid and fervid,
they gazed on time postponed;

safely in the box,
was a timelessly dead clock,
whose hour is now unknown;

voracious sets of eyes,
mouths plying all sorts of lies,
with hearts as cold as a tombstone.

Book Review

Einstein's Beach House
By Jacob Appel
Reviewed by Casey Dorman

Did Einstein own a beach house? With considerable literary license, Jacob Appel suggests that the renowned genius did indeed own such a house, but its exact location remains a mystery. As in several of the stories in his collection, *Einstein's Beach House*, Appel embraces absurdity to the point that reality becomes as ephemeral as possibility. In the title story, a misprint in the AAA guidebook for New Jersey misidentifies the location of the famous physicist's summer residence by transposing the numerals in its address. The owner of the misidentified cottage, taking advantage of the error, begins offering tours of the house. Unfortunately, one of his first customers is a university student who is doing research on Einstein, and when the ersatz tour guide claims that he bought the house from the physicist's niece, the student writes to the niece to inquire further. Somehow, the niece produces a deed to the house, despite its having been in the real owner's family for four generations, and the faux tour guide and his entire family are evicted.

"Paracosmos," is a story in which a young girl develops an obsession with an imaginary friend. When her parents forbid her to "play" with the friend any longer, fearing for her mental health, the girl's mother is visited by the imaginary friend's father, with whom she begins an affair.

Whimsical, paradoxical, absurd?

What these stories, as well as the others in *Einstein's Beach House* have in common is a charmingly playful approach to reality, couched within familiar, often touching, settings involving family and relationships. The author's sense of humor is present, either as foreground or background, in every story, making each a delight to read.

Some themes are repeated. Two of the stories involve taking care of an unusual pet: a box turtle in one and a hedgehog in another, and the consequences of taking such custodial relationships too seriously, so that they dominate the characters' relationships with other humans. In two of the stories the father is portrayed as a fast-talking psychopath who nevertheless devotes his scheming and lying to the welfare of, and in one case to exacting revenge in the name of, his family. Whether such characters are busy duping the public or secretly killing off the relatives of wealthy doctors, they nevertheless come across as human and ultimately lovable.

Throughout the stories, Appel displays a talent for exposing the weaknesses of humans, even in situations where they are presented as irritating, defiant, or vengeful. Often he achieves this by presenting the story through recollections of a child within a family—a child who embodies the innocence and faith in his or her parents that only a child possesses.

What emerges from this collection of stories is a subtle but telling argument for tolerance and understanding, an appreciation of the common human motivations behind what can appear to be aberrant or misguided behavior. And Appel's story-telling skills are considerable. Each story unfolds with an effortless progression, which snares the reader's curiosity, arouses his or her emotions, and makes the story hard to put down. At the close of each story, I found myself pausing to reflect on the emotional insights which had been plumbed within me—but pausing only until my need for reflection was outweighed by my eagerness to begin the next story and see what the author's quirky, original imagination would come up with next.

Einstein's Beach House is published by Pressgang, an affiliate of the MFA in Creative Writing program at Butler University and it won their 2013 Pressgang Prize contest. It is available in paperback.

Poetry

Two Poems by William Miller

Wordsworth's Bucket

He opened the door himself,
offered you a chair
across from his.

He read your letter
of introduction; his wife
brought a tray of tea,

butter and toast. You
hoped to see the poet
who rambled across

the fields of France
during the revolution--
or the bard of Nether Stowey

whose shepherds and peddlers
were heroes of the pasture
remote mountain trails ...

But, he wasn't there, just
an old man disgruntled
by one more pilgrim ...

He didn't understand
the new poets " in love
with easeful death,"

how they fled the country,
as if English bread wasn't
good enough for them ...

You ask the question
you really came this far
to ask. Would he and

Coleridge ever write poems
together, great ballads again?
His answer was to stand up,

Slowly, show you the door.
there was a painted sign
And a bucket on a nail:

"Sir or Madame, kindly pay
for your tea, butter
and toast."

And you had to guess
How much the tea and toast
Of the greatest living

Poet was worth ….
Outside, at least, the lake
Was the same,

choppy from the breeze;
a young man rowed hard.
And there were the hills

where a wanderer told
of a ruined cottage,
beauty in its sad decay.

The Plastic Surgeon's Lament

For years, I peeled faces,
swelled many breasts
with implants.

I made money, bought
everything there was
to buy, loved my
summer house
and pool the best.

But one day, a young
woman, so beautiful,
told me what she wanted
and began to cry.

For once, I asked why,
and she told me her face
was flat, not like
the models with
high cheekbones,
not like them.

I told her she was perfect,
didn't need the table
and blade, to go home
and be happy.

She only smiled and asked
how much, how soon …

Under the hot lights,
I saw that face again,
hesitated, then cut a line—
a scar she'd always see.

I thought she'd cherish
the beauty around it,
the face my knife

didn't touch!

She sued and sued,
won almost everything;
the state took my
license away ...

I live in my summer house,
my only house, room
after empty room.

Sheets on the mirror
keep me from a man
who wants to nick and dye.

I float in my pool
and never read
a glossy magazine,
see the perfect
faces of girls cut before
they're twenty.

Sometimes, I float for hours,
age in the sun
that ages us all,
though money buys
a beautiful corpse.

Poetry

Two Poems by Changming Yuan

Would or Wouldn't: The Variations of the Wing

If every human had a pair of wings
(Made of strong muscles and broad feathers
Rather than wax like Icarus')
Who wouldn't jump high or become eager to fly
Either towards the setting sun
Or against the rising wind?

Who wouldn't migrate afar with sunshine
And glide most straight to a warmer spot
In the open space? Indeed

Who would continue to confine himself
Within the thick walls of a small rented room?

Who would willingly take a detour
Bump into a stranger, or stumble down
Along the way? More important

Who would remain fixed here
At the same corner all her life
Like a rotten stump, hopeless
Of a new green growth?

On Another Rainy Day

Again, water splashing against walls
And windows with each car
Passing by, colored umbrellas moving
Above unidentifiable human legs
Red light blinking towards the storm and
White noise, every cherry tree skeleton
Trying hard to find a shelter, a long-necked man
Hopping around with yesterday's
Vancouver Sun on top off his bald head
An oversized truck full of
Thick cement pipes making a large turn
As a bus is waiting for strangers
To get off or on

Short Story

If Only…
By Heidi C. Bowerman

"If she does it again, she's dead," is how the text read.

If she stopped breathing again is what "it" meant.

Apparently, an oxygen mask was too much to ask for their dying mother. My nieces had somewhere better to be … in New York City.

There was not time enough to drive. They would have to fly out from New Mexico that night. They had somewhere to be … in New York City.

The remains would have to be sent and any service arrangements delayed, indefinitely. Although it would have been nice to commemorate what would have been Natalie's 75th birthday, they may never come back from New York City.

If only they had flown in the first place.

But, Natalie wanted to admire the countryside. She had done it in the past. She was not that much younger then. Besides, she felt fine when they left California.

In Santa Fe, however, the altitude changed. Natalie began to wheeze, uncontrollably.

So they stopped the van, at the nearest emergency room, surprisingly.

"What's wrong with her?" they asked.

"I don't know. It could just be that she's old," the intern said. "What she needs is an IV and an oxygen mask."

"Would you prescribe antibiotics for the road?"

"No!"

"But, we have to be in New York City."

"Does she have an advanced directive?"

"No."

The intern handed them a standard form to sign. The box clearly checked read: do not resuscitate.

As they signed the DNR, Natalie drifted in and out of consciousness. But when she was awake, I imagined her eyes saying, "I don't want to die. Please help me."

Unfortunately, my nieces were too busy planning their itinerary.

Natalie gasped for air.

"She's coding!"

"She's gone."

What may have seemed quick probably was not for Natalie.

But, there would be no time to grieve. The sisters had a plane to catch.

They arrived with what they feared was only a moment to spare before the delivery.

Actually, they were quite early. As it would turn out, the baby came late. Days late. A healthy newborn girl.

"It's too bad grandma couldn't be here," the baby's mother said to my niece.

"Yes. But, like the doctor said, it was just her time to go."

Poetry

Two Poems by Peycho Kanev

The Twin

He is inside me
and with me
from the day
I was born.

We think
the same things
about our world.
I got my face,
but he is in control of
my brain.

And even more!
When we walk under
the sun his shadow
is thicker than mine.
"How is this possible?"
I ask my self.
He says nothing.

He never says anything
at all. He's mute as a mule.
Yet women adore him.
They follow him through
the streets with hollow eyes.

We sleep together at night,
and he dreams my dreams.
But when I wake up
we are the same person again.

And I'm sure it will last
forever. Unless I do something

about that. So I decided
to take him for a walk.

I took him to the fields.
And when I showed him
the scarecrow he began
to tremble with fear.

Ah, the way he screamed in pain.

At the End

At the end of a long day
everything around breathes again,
tranquility hangs,
like a pendulum above the ground.

But that's good, I say. Let it rest.
The greenery, the crosses on the tops
of the churches pointing to heaven,
darkness sneaking behind the mountain,
bringing new life to the creatures
of the night.

At night the stones speak. But not everyone
understands them. Not everyone has the dictionary
of the centuries. But those who have it may hear
the darkest story. It begins anew each day.

Commentary

Religious Freedom or Religious Folly?
The Editor-in-Chief

The Religious Freedom Restoration Act passed by Congress in the 1990's is a law that places the burden upon the government to prove that restricting someone's freedom to practice his or her religion is necessary for the public's protection. Under that act, a person can fight the government in court if that person believes that the government violated his or her religious rights. When the law was passed in 1993, it was meant to preserve the rights of Native Americans to continue using land that they deemed sacred for religious ceremonies, such as burials, despite government efforts to use such lands for public projects. It also protected the rights of Native Americans to use peyote in some of their rituals, despite peyote being a substance banned from use by the government. Its most relevant provision asserted that "government shall not substantially burden a person's exercise of religion even if the burden results from a rule of general applicability," meaning that a federal law does not need to be aimed at a particular group and can apply to the general population, but if it "substantially burdened a person's exercise of religion" it can be set aside for that person or group. Only in cases of "compelling government interest" can the RFRA be overruled. However, it only applies to federal laws, which is why twenty states have their own versions of the law.

Now, both Indiana and Arkansas have enacted their versions of the RFRA, causing an unprecedented furor among both LBGT anti-discrimination advocates and many private businesses. Initially, defenders of the new state laws claimed that there was no difference between their states' laws and the federal law, which had been sponsored by Democrat Chuck Schumer and passed by President Bill Clinton with strong bipartisan support (including support by then-state senator Barack Obama). Opponents within the two states cited the motivation behind the passage of these new state laws, which they claimed was the desire of conservative religious groups to find a legal reason to discriminate against gays and lesbians. They also pointed to the fact that the laws concerned the religious rights of businesses, rather than individuals, as in the federal law, and that they allowed use of the law in defense against lawsuits by private individuals, not just the government, as the federal law stipulates.

Both sides in the debate were being disingenuous. While it is true that conservative religious groups were the main supporters of these new RFRA laws, it is not true that the federal law only applies to the religious freedoms of individuals. The Supreme Court's Hobby Lobby decision, which was about the federal RFRA made it clear that closely-held private businesses have the same religious rights as individuals with regard to the federal law. The Indiana and Arkansas laws simply reflected that decision. But that did not make the Indiana and Arkansas laws carbon copies of the federal law. The federal RFRA still cannot be invoked except in the case of a government regulation restricting the religious rights of either a person or a private corporation, while the state laws allowed them to be used against a lawsuit brought by an individual or private group. This remained a difference between the federal and these two states' RFRA statutes and it is an important one, since it meant that businesses which assert their right to refuse service to someone on the basis of religious freedom need not fear that that person can bring a civil lawsuit against them.

The United States prides itself on being a pluralistic society with regard to religion. Our founding fathers were particularly sensitive to the interference of the government in religious matters. We have no state-sponsored religion and all religions are equally protected under our laws and our constitution. The RFRA is part of the fabric of laws that protect our religious freedom. In France, it is illegal for school girls to wear headscarves to school, because that is a sign of affirmation of the Muslim faith, which many Frenchmen feel creates an unhealthy division within their society. No such law could be passed in the United States. Even if it were argued that having unique clothing styles among different religious groups undermines national solidarity and erodes social capital, the RFRA would not allow such laws as were passed in France to be put in place in the United States. Neither can Jews be forced to remove their kippahs or Amish to shave their beards. So before urging the government to throw out the RFRA, we need to think about the reasons it's there.

On the other hand, a new wave of "religious freedom" seems to be sweeping across parts of the United States. Indiana and Arkansas passed their own versions of the RFRA, which extended the law in states in which gay, lesbian, bisexual and transgender individuals are not included in anti-discrimination laws—states such as Indiana and

Arkansas. Fourteen other states have had similar legislation introduced to be voted on during the next year. By itself, this is not new and can even be applauded. The Supreme Court ruled that the federal law does not apply to states, so each state must pass its own law in order to have the same protection for religious freedoms ensconced in the federal statute. Twenty states have already done so. But taking a cue from the Supreme Court's Hobby Lobby decision, Indiana and Arkansas are now including private businesses as well as individuals in terms of the definition of "persons" practicing their religions. In addition, in these two states the new laws allow the state's RFRA law to be used as a defense in a legal suit by an individual, rather than in a defense against a government entity, which has violated a person's religious freedom. This last difference, which is found elsewhere only in the Texas RFRA, further raised peoples' fears that the law could be used to defend discriminatory practices in business (note that at the time of this writing, Governors of both states were seeking to change the laws to make them less able to be used to discriminate against anyone).

Governors in both Indiana and Arkansas, aware of the backlash their proposed laws created across the nation and within their own states' business communities, demanded that anti-discrimination guarantees be added to their RFRA statutes. While this is not "too little, too late," as some have claimed, that the governors had to defy their own state legislatures to force such alterations in their laws is an indictment against the mindset of conservative religious groups.

Although discrimination against a person on the basis of his or her religion was one of the main reasons anti-discrimination laws were developed in the United States, with the gradual liberalization of attitudes toward race and sexuality, some religiously minded people have come to feel that having to accept legitimization of practices to which they feel their religious beliefs are opposed, has become a violation of their religious freedom. This has included, at first, such things as integration of the races, then interracial marriage and now contraception, abortion, and same sex marriage.

Given that there are some people who disapprove of same sex marriage, or of the use of contraception or of abortion on the basis of their religious beliefs, it certainly seems valid that no one, either the government or their fellow citizens, has the right to force them to accept such practices *for themselves* (it is not clear what this could even mean with regard to same sex marriage). But what about in the public sphere? Does their religious freedom extend to how we treat people in our business dealings? According to the Supreme Court it does.

But isn't observing one's religion a personal behavior? Even if it involves observing holidays not observed by the majority of citizens, or restricting one's eating habits, or dressing or speaking in a certain way (some Quakers still say "thee" and "thy"), these behaviors seem more personal than refusing to serve someone else, or providing her some types of healthcare. When does observing one's religion slide over into imposing that religion's values upon someone else? Sure, there are always other places to work, or to buy wedding cakes or flowers, but that argument begs the question. And the question is— when does observing one's religious beliefs in one's business practices become discrimination?

In the case of the Hobby Lobby decision, although it is clearly an instance in which personal religious beliefs are being allowed to determine how a business owner treats his or her employees, there appears to be no case for claiming discrimination. Not providing contraception in a health care plan applies equally to everyone and is not a decision made on the basis of characteristics of the employee (except perhaps that it applies to women not to men, but then that's true of lots of medical services. Medicare does not pay for medications to treat erectile dysfunction, but that's not discriminatory against men even though the rule applies to men only.) But in the case of providing services to someone whose personal behaviors violate one's religious beliefs, e.g. gays or lesbians, this certainly appears to be discriminatory because the same services *are* being provided to others.

So something is wrong. In what sense can providing a service to someone else—a service that one feels perfectly fine providing to others—compromise one's religious rights? In what sense can refusing to provide that service to someone on the basis of his or her sexual orientation not be discrimination pure and simple? In fact it *is* discrimination and no one's religious rights are being compromised by providing such services. The real reason for enacting such a law as Indiana first enacted and Arkansas almost enacted, was to send a message about conservative religious groups' disapproval of gay, lesbian and bisexual behavior, including marriage. That's a message that was already quite apparent. What these groups wanted to add was punishment to those in the LBGT community who want to be open about their sexual preferences and practices. The message now was "If you're LBGT and you want to live in our community, you are going to live uncomfortably." In other words, you're not welcome here.

Is this the kind of message that religion teaches us to send to our fellow Americans?

Submissions

Submission Guidelines – Short Stories, Poetry, Reviews, etc.

Lost Coast Review welcomes unsolicited submissions of short stories, poetry, book reviews, film reviews, photography or art (Must be black and white to appear in the paperback version of *Lost Coast Review*. Color art may appear in the online version only.) Commentary on artistic and sociopolitical topics is also occasionally accepted, if it is of superior merit. *Lost Coast Review* does not pay authors for their work.

Guidelines:

1. It may take awhile to get back to you. So please be patient.

2. Submissions by email only. Include a brief description of your work in the body of the email, including the category (short story, poem, book review, film review, commentary, art or photography). Attach the work itself as a Word document (.doc or .docx) or, if art, as a jpeg.

3. We normally limit poetry to no more than three poems per issue by a single poet and short stories to 4,000 words or less.

4. Please include your name, contact information, and previous publishing history or any kind of credits that could be interesting to readers. Include these at the end of your submission.

5. If your piece is accepted, we will proofread and edit it. If anything further than that is necessary, we will first run changes by you for your final approval.

6. By submitting an item, you grant us your consent to publish it in *Lost Coast Review*. The *Review* asks only for the right to publish a story or poem for the first time, on the Web and in print. All rights revert to the author after publication by *Lost Coast Review*. All accepted work will be archived on the *Lost Coast Review* website.

7. If you want to submit your material elsewhere in the meantime, that's fine. Just be sure to let us know if it gets published somewhere else before we've had a chance to respond.

8. You may withdraw your submission prior to publication by contacting us and identifying the item by title and author.

9. By submitting material, you are acknowledging that you solely own the copyright and agree to the above guidelines.

10. Use the email address below to submit work and label it *submission*.

Contact Us: Our email address is: info@avignonpress.com

www.ingramcontent.com/pod-product-compliance
Lightning Source LLC
Chambersburg PA
CBHW051044030426
42339CB00006B/188